Sexual Dysfunction in Men

About the Author

David L. Rowland received his PhD from the University of Chicago in 1977, and since then has held numerous research fellowships in the US and abroad. His research focuses on understanding sexual response and disorders in men and women, particularly the interface between the physiological and psychological experience of sexual response. He has published over 130 articles, monographs, and chapters, including the 2008 *Handbook of Sexual and Gender Identity Disorders*. He served as editor of the *Annual Review of Sex Research*, 2005–2009, currently serves on the editorial boards of major journals in the field of sex research, and has provided expert consultation to pharmaceutical companies and professional societies, including service on the Standards Committee of the International Society of Sexual Medicine.

Companion volume in this series:

Marta Meana (2012)
Sexual Dysfunction in Women
ISBN 978-0-88937-400-3

Advances in Psychotherapy – Evidence-Based Practice

Series Editor
Danny Wedding, PhD, MPH, Professor of Psychology, California School of Professional
    Psychology / Alliant International University, San Francisco, CA

Associate Editors
Larry Beutler, PhD, Professor, Palo Alto University / Pacific Graduate School of Psychology,
    Palo Alto, CA
Kenneth E. Freedland, PhD, Professor of Psychiatry and Psychology, Washington University
    School of Medicine, St. Louis, MO
Linda C. Sobell, PhD, ABPP, Professor, Center for Psychological Studies, Nova Southeastern
    University, Ft. Lauderdale, FL
David A. Wolfe, PhD, RBC Chair in Children's Mental Health, Centre for Addiction and Mental
    Health, University of Toronto, ON

The basic objective of this series is to provide therapists with practical, evidence-based treatment guidance for the most common disorders seen in clinical practice – and to do so in a "reader-friendly" manner. Each book in the series is both a compact "how-to" reference on a particular disorder for use by professional clinicians in their daily work, as well as an ideal educational resource for students and for practice-oriented continuing education.

The most important feature of the books is that they are practical and "reader-friendly:" All are structured similarly and all provide a compact and easy-to-follow guide to all aspects that are relevant in real-life practice. Tables, boxed clinical "pearls," marginal notes, and summary boxes assist orientation, while checklists provide tools for use in daily practice.

Sexual Dysfunction in Men

David L. Rowland
Department of Psychology, Valparaiso University, Valparaiso, IN

HOGREFE

Library of Congress Cataloging in Publication

is available via the Library of Congress Marc Database under the
Library of Congress Control Number 2012904633

Library and Archives Canada Cataloguing in Publication

Rowland, David L.
    Sexual dysfunction in men / David L. Rowland.

(Advances in psychotherapy--evidence-based practice ; 26)
Includes bibliographical references.
ISBN 978-0-88937-402-7

    1. Sexual disorders. 2. Psychosexual disorders. 3. Men--
Sexual behavior. I. Title. II. Series: Advances in psychotherapy--
evidence-based practice ; 26.

RC556.R69 2012   616.85'8300811   C2012-901983-6

PUBLISHING OFFICES
USA: Hogrefe Publishing, 875 Massachusetts Avenue, 7th Floor, Cambridge, MA 02139
                Phone (866) 823-4726, Fax (617) 354-6875; E-mail customerservice@hogrefe-publishing.com
EUROPE: Hogrefe Publishing, Merkelstr. 3, 37085 Göttingen, Germany
                Phone +49 551 99950-0, Fax +49 551 99950-425, E-mail publishing@hogrefe.com

SALES & DISTRIBUTION
USA: Hogrefe Publishing, Customer Services Department,
                30 Amberwood Parkway, Ashland, OH 44805
                Phone (800) 228-3749, Fax (419) 281-6883, E-mail customerservice@hogrefe.com
EUROPE: Hogrefe Publishing, Merkelstr. 3, 37085 Göttingen, Germany
                Phone +49 551 99950-0, Fax +49 551 99950-425, E-mail publishing@hogrefe.com

OTHER OFFICES
CANADA: Hogrefe Publishing, 660 Eglinton Ave. East, Suite 119-514, Toronto, Ontario, M4G 2K2
SWITZERLAND: Hogrefe Publishing, Länggass-Strasse 76, CH-3000 Bern 9

Hogrefe Publishing
Incorporated and registered in the Commonwealth of Massachusetts, USA, and in Göttingen, Lower Saxony,
Germany

Printed and bound in the USA
ISBN: 978-0-88937-402-7

Preface

The past decade has witnessed increased interest in and research on sexual problems in both men and women. At the same time, new pharmacological solutions to male sexual dysfunctions have become available, and a number of new agents are currently under investigation. These developments are, of course, not independent of one another, but in the course of these developments, two things have become apparent:

(1) We are still far from having a complete understanding of basic human sexual response, let alone sexual dysfunction. For example, we do not understand why some men seem unable to control or delay their ejaculation, or why other men are particularly vulnerable to developing "performance anxiety," while others do not quickly lose their erections as a result of experiencing a sexual problem.

(2) Contrary to speculation that psychosexual counseling would become obsolete (given this pills-for-better-sex decade), its role has actually become better understood and defined. If nothing else, this decade has taught us that although pills can help fix the body and genitals, psychosexual counseling is needed to help heal both the person and the relationship.

This book is written for a broad audience that includes not only nonspecialist therapists, clinicians, and even physicians whose patients/clients raise concerns about their sexual well-being, but also for patients/clients themselves and their partners. Although some sexual problems invariably require the attention of a specialist, many others can be handled adequately by the nonspecialist assuming (1) he or she already has training as a therapist or clinician and (2) he or she has acquired a reasonably broad understanding of men's sexual dysfunctions – their etiologies, diagnoses, and treatments. Meeting these assumptions ensures that the therapist's general counseling skills are contextualized and tailored to meet the needs of clients who express a sexual concern or difficulty.

It is indeed the second assumption above that has provided the impetus for this book. Many therapists may not feel qualified or comfortable dealing with the sexual problems of clients. Together with its twin, *Sexual Dysfunction in Women,* authored by Marta Meana, these volumes not only give general frameworks for thinking about sexual response and sexual problems, but also set forth diagnostic and treatment strategies in a simplified and clear manner for the nonspecialist.

Acknowledgments

I am grateful to all who made this book possible: Marta who suggested the collaboration, Danny Wedding, the series editor, and Robert Dimbleby of Hogrefe Publishers.

Special thanks go to Beth Adamski, MA, editorial assistant for this project, who was instrumental in both task and stress management; to Paula Nieweem, MALS, who carried out research and investigation for the book; and to Kathleen Mullen, PhD, whose rhetorical eye and ear have helped ensure a smooth and easy read.

And finally, to those who continue to enrich my life: my daughter, parents, special friends left unnamed, and the staff of the Graduate School and Office of Continuing Education at Valparaiso University.

Table of Contents

1

Description

The ability to have a fulfilling sexual relationship is important to almost all men's mental health and psychological well-being. Not only is this a biologically and socially defining characteristic for men in our society, but studies suggest that men in such relationships tend to have greater longevity and to report a higher quality of life and overall satisfaction (McCabe, 1997; Palmore, 1985). Men whose sexual relationships are disrupted because of their inability to respond adequately, typically experience a number of psychological symptoms, including lack of confidence, anxiety, and distress.

Although a select few therapists specialize in the treatment of sexual problems, most do not; therefore, the likelihood that a client or patient may approach a general therapist who counsels and treats patients with a variety of issues is quite high. Even the generalist can be helpful to men in need of sexual guidance and advice. Important to this process is an understanding of the components of sexual response, its etiology and diagnosis, and current treatment practices.

Even the nonspecialized therapist can be helpful by understanding the etiology, diagnosis, and treatment practices for various dysfunctions

1.1 Terminology

Sexual response is complex: It requires specific preconditions, involves multiple behavioral responses, and includes an array of psychosocial factors that have affective, cognitive, and relationship dimensions. Masters and Johnson (1966) succeeded in providing a rudimentary characterization of physiological sexual response, analyzing it into arousal, plateau, orgasmic, and resolution phases. Subsequent models introduced a role for *sexual desire* as a component of sexual response (Kaplan, 1979), with a more recent refinement that distinguishes between such constructs as *spontaneous desire* and *arousability*, the latter referring to sexual interest derived from a specific individual, object, or context as opposed to an "unprompted" desire. Further conceptualization has included separate pain-pleasure dimensions (Schover, Friedman, Weiler, Heiman, & LoPiccolo, 1982), as well as attention to other subjective factors such as the feelings, motivations, and attitudes that surround the sexual act (Byrne & Schulte, 1990). Recently, emphasis has also been given to the role of the dyadic relationship, an approach that seeks to understand and treat sexual dysfunction in its relational context (Schnarch, 1988, 1991).

Healthy sexual relationships, however, are not characterized merely by the absence of dysfunctional response. Key elements of healthy sexual relationships include passion, intimacy and caring, and commitment (Sternberg & Barnes, 1988).

Healthy sexual relationships involve more than just the absence of dysfunctional response; many problems include larger relationship factors beyond sexual response issues

- Passion typically involves such characteristics as sexual feelings, physical attraction, and romantic love.
- Intimacy and caring deal with dimensions of affection and expressiveness – the willingness to communicate and share beliefs, attitudes, and feelings.
- Commitment refers to the decision to be with one partner and to work hard to maintain the relationship.

Because many sexual problems are rooted in a couple's disparate expectations and emotional struggles, including the different ways in which these elements are often played out by each of the sexes, most sexual problems benefit not just from attention to specific sexual response issues but to larger relationship factors as well.

There are several different types of sexual disorders. In the field of sexology, distinctions are made among the sexual dysfunctions, the gender identity disorders, and atypical and paraphilic behaviors.

- *Sexual dysfunction* refers to disruption or inadequacy of normal sexual responding and is the topic of this book.
- *Gender identity disorders* refer to cross-gender identity or the lack of assimilation of, or satisfaction with, the gender identity consistent with one's biological sex or assigned gender identity.
- *Paraphilias* refer to sexual arousal and behaviors that are directed toward inappropriate objects/partners or are carried out in inappropriate situations (e.g., fetishism, pedophilia, frotteurism, voyeurism, etc.).

1.2   Definition

The classification of sexual dysfunctions has evolved from the conceptual models discussed above and is related to the specific axes or dimensions important to functional sexual response (American Psychiatric Association, 2000). These include:

- lack of desire, also known as hypoactive sexual desire disorder;
- problems with either physiological sexual arousal (e.g., erection) or subjective sexual arousal (i.e., actually feeling aroused);
- disorders of ejaculation/orgasm, most commonly premature ejaculation and inhibited ejaculation.

Although not part of this review, problems with painful intercourse and sexual aversion are also included in the diagnostic classification system.

Typically, the scope of the sexual problem is characterized as either situation- (including person) specific or generalized, and as either lifelong or acquired. An acquired sexual dysfunction may result from either pathophysiological developments or sexual experiences. Several classification systems are currently in use to define and characterize sexual dysfunctions: The American Psychiatric Association's *Diagnostic and Statistical Manual of Mental Disorders*, 4th Edition, Text Revision (DSM-IV-TR), the proposed 5th edition of the DSM (DSM-5), and the *International Statistical Classification of Diseases and Related Health Problems*, 10th Edition (ICD-10) classifications are included in Table 1. Characteristics of each dysfunction, along with alternate terminology and prevalence estimates are provided in Table 2.

Table 1
Comparison of Terminology Across Diagnostic Manuals for Sexual Dysfunctions in Men

DSM-IV-TR (codes)	ICD-10 (codes)	DSM-5 proposed (as of May 15, 2011)
Sexual Desire Disorders		
HSDD (302.71)	Loss or lack of sexual desire (F52.0)	*Hypoactive sexual desire disorder in men*
Sexual Arousal Disorders		
Male erectile disorder (302.72)	Failure of genital response (F52.2)	*Erectile disorder*
Orgasm Disorders		
MOD (302.74)	Orgasmic dysfunction (F52.3)	*Delayed ejaculation*
Premature ejaculation (302.75)	Premature ejaculation (F52.4)	*Early ejaculation*

Note. DSM-IV-TR = *Diagnostic and Statistical Manual of Mental Disorders,* 4th Edition, Text Revision (APA, 2000); HSDD = Hypoactive sexual desire disorder; ICD-10 = *International Statistical Classification of Diseases and Related Health Problems,* 10th Edition (World Health Organization, 1992); MOD = Male orgasmic disorder.

Although sexual dysfunctions in men and women generally parallel one another, the prevalence of the various dysfunctions differentiates the sexes; and, because of differences in physiology and evolution, they are often manifested in different ways (Lewis et al., 2004). For example, anorgasmia and lack of sexual desire are more common among women, whereas rapid ejaculation/ orgasm and physiological arousal problems (e.g., erection in men versus lubrication in women) are more common among men.

In broad terms, no matter what the problem, men's sexual problems typically have three elements:

(1) A *functional impairment* of some type is evident. For example, the man and his partner are unable to enjoy intercourse because he is unable to get or keep an erection, or because he ejaculates very quickly.

(2) The man's sense of *self-efficacy is low*, as he is typically unable to correct or control the problem through psychobehavioral changes. For example, the man just cannot seem to get interested in sex, or he is unable to delay his ejaculation.

(3) The man and/or his partner suffer *negative consequences* from the condition. For example, the man is bothered or even obsessed by the problem, perhaps to the point of avoiding intimacy; or the partner is distressed by the situation, not knowing what to do, perhaps feeling frustrated and unattractive, and so on. The challenge in the field of sexology, however, is that although there is only "one" unified sexual response in the patient's view – the man typically does not distinguish among the desire, erection, and ejaculation phases of the response – the physiology underlying the functional impairment associated with each

The functional impairment associated with each phase of the sexual response cycle has a distinct underlying physiology

Table 2
Definition and Prevalence of Major Male Sexual Dysfunctions

Dysfunction/nomenclature		Defining characteristics	DSM-IV code	Pre-valence	Age[a]
Hypoactive sexual desire disorder (HSDD)	Loss of libido or sexual interest	– Diminished/absent interest of desire – Absent sexual thoughts or fantasies – Lack of responsive desire	302.71	4–25%	++
Arousal disorder[b]		– No or diminished subjective erotic feelings despite normal erection	302.70	NA	
Erectile dysfunction (ED)	Impotence	– Inability to attain erection – Inability to maintain erection to completion of activity – Coital penetration impaired ≥ 50%	302.72	10–45%	+++
Premature ejaculation (PE)	Rapid ejaculation Early ejaculation	– Onset of orgasm and ejaculation before or shortly after penetration – Ejaculation within 1 min or less – Occurs before desired due to lack of control	302.75	12–30%	?
Male orgasmic disorder (MOD)	Ejaculatory incompe-tence Retarded or delayed ejaculation Inhibited ejaculation	– Delayed or absent orgasm following normal excitement (erection) phase	302.74	5–10%	++
Dyspareunia		– Pain associated with intercourse before, during, or after	302.76	1–5%	

Note. DSM-IV = *Diagnostic and Statistical Manual of Mental Disorders,* 4th Edition.
[a]Indicates whether the dysfunction increases with age in a weak (+), moderate (++), or strong (+++) manner.
[b]Subjective arousal disorder does not have a dedicated classification but is increasingly recognized as a potential problem for men with orgasmic disorders.
Adapted from "Sexual Health and Problems: Erectile Dysfunction, Premature Ejaculation, and Orgasmic Disorders," by D. L. Rowland, in J. Grant & M. Potenza (Eds.), *Textbook of Men's Mental Health* (pp. 171–204). Arlington, VA: American Psychiatric Association Press, 2007.

of these phases is quite distinct. Thus, dysfunction within each phase has its own prevalence, etiology, diagnosis, and treatment. To provide greater depth and understanding, this book takes a dual approach, dealing with common and comprehensive issues underlying all dysfunctions in Chapters 1–3, and then devoting individual sections to each phase/dysfunction in Chapter 4.

1.3   Epidemiology

For obvious reasons, determining the prevalence of any sexual dysfunction in men is complicated and challenging. To illustrate the point, defining a problem as a sexual *dysfunction* requires that the functional impairment meet specific criteria. In many instances, a man may view his response as problematic, but it may not meet the criteria necessary for a clinical diagnosis. For example, a man has occasional erectile failure, or ejaculates before he wants to even when ejaculation occurs 3 or 4 minutes after vaginal insertion. Furthermore, for a man to be classified as dysfunctional also requires that he recognize the symptoms and potentially defines himself in this category. Yet, issues of privacy, discretion, and sometimes stigmatization may inhibit men from disclosing what might be viewed as a "weakness" (what man wants to admit to being classified as *dys*functional?). Finally, prevalence is a moving target. For example, for some men, the problem may be transient, as when life stressors or particular sensitivity or vulnerability to specific relationship interactions contribute to or intensify a problem that is initially "subclinical." Cultural attitudes, expectations, and acceptance regarding men's sexual problems may influence the willingness to acknowledge and report such problems. And for those sexual dysfunctions that are partly age-related (e.g., problems with erection and/or sometimes sexual interest), as the age demographic of a population changes, so also does the prevalence (see Table 2 for prevalence estimates).

Many factors contribute to the difficulty of determining the prevalence of sexual dysfunctions in men

Men may be hesitant to identify themselves as dysfunctional, since classification as "dysfunctional" is stigmatizing and requires their recognition of the symptoms

1.3.1   Low Sexual Desire

Data from the National Health and Social Life Survey (Laumann, Paik, & Rosen, 1999) suggest the prevalence of low sexual desire is around 5%. This particular survey had several limitations, and the more recent Global Study of Sexual Attitudes and Behaviors (Laumann, Nicolosi, Glasser, Paik, & Gingell, 2005) suggests a higher prevalence, somewhere between 13% and 28%. Given the general superiority of this latter survey, these rates are probably more reflective of the true prevalence. Several other studies report rates ranging from 0 to about 25%, depending on the nature of the question, the population sampled, and whether the individuals were clinically- or self-diagnosed. Taken together, these and other studies (Lewis et al., 2010) suggest prevalence somewhere between 15% and 25% of men, with the potential of higher rates in men over 60. However, most such studies have not distinguished between

It is important to distinguish between sexual *desire* and sexual *interest*

sexual "desire" and "interest." Whereas desire is presumed to be internally driven and physiologically based (at least for men), *interest* is a more inclusive term that may be affected by such factors as partner attraction, relationship issues, environmental stressors, and so on. The extent to which this more inclusive condition (low sexual "interest") prevails in the population is not known despite the fact that low sexual interest undoubtedly affects the sexual relationship.

1.3.2   Erectile Dysfunction

Prevalence of erectile dysfunction (ED) among men varies significantly according to the way in which the dysfunction is defined, the population sampled, and information collected (Lewis et al., 2010). Overall, an estimated 18% of males 20 years and older, or about 18 million men in the United States, have erectile dysfunction (Selvin, Burnett, & Platz, 2007). However, the most important source of variation in ED prevalence is the age of the respondents. Among men below the age of 40, ED ranges from 1% to 10%; for those between 40 and 49, ED is higher, perhaps closer to 8–12%; for those 50 or older, the prevalence approaches 25% and can reach as high as 50%+ for men in their 70s and 80s. Clearly, the age-related increase in prevalence strongly suggests an ED of somatic/biogenic origin; reliable estimates regarding the prevalence of psychogenic ED are not available.

The prevalence of biogenic ED is easier to estimate than psychogenic ED, as the age-related increase offers evidence of a biogenic origin

Undoubtedly, the link between biogenic and psychogenic ED is important – as men experience increased difficulty getting and maintaining an erection due to biogenic factors, they are more likely to experience anxiety and performance demand, two psychological factors that interfere with erectile response. Nevertheless, such links between biogenic and psychogenic factors may not necessarily presume higher levels of psychogenic ED in older men. Just as readily, younger men having limited experience with sexual intimacy, entering new relationships, or having to deal with strongly defined social roles are also vulnerable to the antierectile effects of anxiety and performance demand within a sexual relationship.

1.3.3   Premature Ejaculation

PE is probably the most common sexual dysfunction in men

Premature ejaculation (PE) appears to be fairly common; in fact, it is probably the most common sexual dysfunction in the general population, including primary care patients, with studies reporting ranges from 11% to 66% (Ahn et al., 2007; Aschka, Himmel, Ittner, & Kochen, 2001). Most studies estimate 20–30% of men, regardless of nationality, will experience PE at some point in their lives (see Rowland, 2011). Variability in estimates likely arises from:
(1) the use of different definitions of premature ejaculation, particularly definitions for the latency to ejaculation, which has ranged anywhere from one to several minutes after partner penetration;
(2) whether the estimate is based on a clinical diagnosis versus self-report by the responder;

(3) the extent to which the man is actually bothered by the condition. Several studies, for example, report rates as high as 30%, but only half those men indicate the problem is sufficiently serious to seek treatment.

As expected, prevalence estimates from clinical samples of men attending sex clinics or seeing primary care physicians suggest somewhat higher rates than in the general population (Aschka et al., 2001), with 34.8% of men in one sample reporting having experienced PE at some time during their lifetime (Riley & Riley, 2005). Overall, such data suggest that the rates of PE or PE-like complaints are quite high – probably around 15-25% within the general population. Some research indicates that age is not a factor with respect to the prevalence of PE; other research, however, suggests that PE may either increase or decrease with increasing age (e.g., Ahn et al., 2007). Given the inconsistent results, the most parsimonious position is to assume that there is no *large* change in PE prevalence related to age.

1.3.4   Delayed and Inhibited Ejaculation

The prevalence of delayed or inhibited ejaculation (IE; the latter being the complete inability to reach ejaculation) is unclear – normative data for defining the duration of "normal" ejaculatory latency, particularly regarding the right tail of the distribution (i.e., beyond the mean latency to ejaculation), is essentially nonexistent. Furthermore, larger epidemiological studies have not subdivided men into various types of diminished ejaculatory function. For example, the continuum (and/or overlap) from delayed to inhibited ejaculation has not been adequately explored.

In general, IE has been reported at fairly low rates in the literature, typically around 3% (Rowland et al., 2010), and thus it has been seen as a clinical rarity. Masters and Johnson (1966) initially reported only 17 cases; Apfelbaum (2000) reported 34 cases and Kaplan fewer than 50 cases in their respective practices (see Perelman & Rowland, 2008). However, based on clinical experiences, some urologists and sex therapists are reporting an increasing incidence of IE (Rowland et al., 2010) leading to newer estimates of anywhere between 3% and 10% (see Lewis et al., 2010). The prevalence of IE appears to be moderately and positively related to age – not surprising in view of the fact that ejaculatory function as a whole tends to diminish with age. However, no large-scale studies have systematically investigated the strength or reliability of this putative relationship.

1.3.5   Other Considerations

The various dysfunctions themselves do not represent mutually exclusive categories. In fact, the interrelatedness of the components of the sexual response cycle increases the likelihood that men with a problem related to one phase of the sexual response cycle may exhibit a problem in another phase. Important to any evaluation and treatment process is determining which problem is primary and which is secondary. Thus, a man who has significant problems with erection may eventually "lose" or suppress interest in sex altogether. Similarly,

Due to the interrelatedness of the phases of the sexual response cycle, men with one sexual problem will often manifest other sexual problems

When multiple problems are encountered, it is important to distinguish between which problem is primary and which is secondary

nearly one third of men reporting problems with premature ejaculation also experience difficulties with erection.

Generally, a common underlying theme for all sexual dysfunctions is that they are bothersome and cause significant worry or distress to the individual. In some instances, the distress may not just be caused by inadequate sexual performance, but may stem from the impact the dysfunction has on the couple (e.g., disruption of intimacy, lack of partner satisfaction, etc.). In contrast, some men may experience minimal distress due to their condition. For example, a man who ejaculates very rapidly may employ strategies other than coitus to ensure his partner's sexual enjoyment and therefore may have little distress and consequently little motivation to seek treatment. The question – one that has been debated vigorously in sexological circles – is whether such men, that is, those showing the symptoms but without stress or bother, manifest a true sexual dysfunction.

1.4   Course and Prognosis

1.4.1   Psychophysiology of Male Sexual Function: A Brief Overview

Libido or sexual desire is a psychological construct

To understand risk factors and treatment options, a basic familiarity with the psychophysiological processes of sexual desire, sexual arousal, and orgasm is helpful. *Libido* or *sexual desire* is a psychological construct intended to explain the likelihood or strength of a sexual response. Constructs do not have the same observable qualities as, say, erection or ejaculation, but they are nevertheless presumed to exist and are invoked to explain variations in response frequency and intensity. In men, libido or desire is usually assessed through self-reports of interest in sexual activity and a sexual partner, the presence of self-generated fantasies, and the frequency of sexual activity (coitus, masturbation). At the neural level, libido represents a state of "arousability" that most likely involves "motivation" centers in the diencephalon (e.g., medial preoptic area; paraventricular nucleus of the hypothalamus), operating in conjunction with cortical level sensory and cognitive centers responsible for processing sexually relevant information about the environment (e.g., appropriate partner, appropriate time, etc.) (Pfaus, Kippin, & Coria-Avila, 2003). The presence of androgen, particularly testosterone, appears to be an important modulator of sexual desire in men, "priming" (i.e., lowering the threshold for) neural responsivity under specific contexts/conditions and to sexually relevant stimuli.

Sexual arousal involves both brain and genital activation

Given the appropriate stimulus conditions, the man will respond with *sexual arousal*, a process that involves both central (brain) and genital activation. The precise brain mechanisms for arousal appear to be centered in the hypothalamic and limbic areas, but whole brain processing of contextual stimuli (sensory input), emotional state (positive or negative), and past experience/future consequences (probable frontal lobe contribution) is important to the process. Arousal most probably involves autonomic (sympathetic?) activation (giving rise to "erotic feelings") integrated with the aforementioned "motivation" and cognitive processing centers that then regulate the descending neural impulses responsible for penile response.

Penile erection is a vascular process involving increased arterial inflow to the penis, penile engorgement with blood, and decreased venous outflow from the organ, processes that result in sufficient rigidity for sexual intercourse (Lue, 1992). Whether the penis is erect or flaccid depends upon the physiology of corporal cavernosal smooth muscle tone, that is, the equilibrium between proerectile and antierectile mechanisms controlling, respectively, relaxant and contractile responses of the smooth muscle cells comprising the penile blood vessels and cavernous tissue. Specifically, the erect penis results from *relaxation* of smooth muscle cells – the vasculature (arteries, arterioles, and capillaries) in the penis opens to allow the increased flow necessary for engorgement. The flaccid penis is characterized by *contraction* of smooth muscle cells – constricted vasculature limits the blood flow to the penis (Burnett, 1999).

In response to the descending neural innervation (probably parasympathetic), a number of events occur at the target *cell membrane* and the *intracellular level*. Specifically, second messenger molecules (e.g., cyclic guanosine monophosphate [cGMP] or cyclic adenosine monophosphate [cAMP]) and ions carry out the neural signal via the action of receptor proteins at the cell membrane of the target cell (e.g., smooth muscle) or via enzyme pathways. Regarding the latter process, these enzymatic pathways (e.g., phosphodiesterase) within the muscle cell may inactivate various pathways and therefore inhibit erectile function. Indeed, medications for erectile dysfunction (e.g., sildenafil [Viagra]) operate through these pathways. Such agents inhibit phosphodiesterase-5 (PDE-5), the enzyme that deactivates cGMP, the energy-consuming process that stimulates relaxation of corporal cavernosal tissue (and thus erection). As a result, cGMP remains active in increasing amounts to exert corporal smooth muscle relaxant effects (Boolel et al., 1996). Stated simply, these prosexual drugs for ED act by inhibiting the system that inhibits erection at the level of penile tissue.

Prosexual drugs for ED act by inhibiting the system that inhibits erection at the level of penile tissue

Ejaculation represents the sequencing of two reflexes under cerebral control that typically coincide with the high point of sexual arousal (Motofei & Rowland, 2005a; Rowland & Slob, 1997). Unlike erection, which may occur in the absence of direct penile stimulation, the ejaculatory reflexes generally require penile stimulation. The first reflex – emission – is a sympathetic response that closes the bladder neck (preventing urination and retrograde ejaculation) and stimulates excretion of seminal fluid (which mixes with sperm) from the prostate into the urethral tract. This first stage of ejaculation is associated with the "ejaculatory inevitability" that men experience prior to actual expulsion of the seminal fluid, and serves as the trigger for the second reflex. The second reflex – putatively involving the parasympathetic system and/or somatic motor system – involves the expulsion of the seminal fluid from the urethra, achieved through the rhythmic contractions of the bulbocavernosal and ischiocavernosal muscles (associated with anal sphincter muscle contraction). The subjective (brain) perception of these contractions, mediated through sensory neurons in the region, gives rise to the experience of orgasm, which comprises a distinct and separate loop. Thus, ejaculation can and does (rarely) occur without concomitant orgasm.

Subjective (brain) perceptions of the contractions that lead to the expulsion of seminal fluid lead to the experience of orgasm

Serotonin has been implicated in the trigger for ejaculation. Various anti-depressant drugs that affect the serotonin have been used to treat premature ejaculation

The mechanism that actually triggers the entire ejaculatory process is not well understood, but the brain neurotransmitter serotonin has been implicated. Accordingly, various antidepressant drugs that affect the serotonergic system – for example, tricyclics (Anafranil) and selective serotonin reuptake inhibitors (SSRIs [Prozac, Zoloft, etc.]) have been used fairly effectively to prolong intercourse in men who usually ejaculate very rapidly. Not surprisingly, since ejaculation is also mediated in part by the sympathetic nervous system, prescription and over-the-counter drugs that attenuate sympathetic response (and there are dozens) may interfere with a normal ejaculatory process.

The above summary makes it clear that the basic rudiments of sexual response are complex and not fully understood. Furthermore, it underscores the many possible points at which the process can go awry. Given the high level of psychophysiological integration required for coordinated sexual response, it is not surprising that sexual response, important as it is to procreation, is sensitive to a myriad of physiological and psychological factors.

1.4.2   Etiology of Male Sexual Dysfunction

Causes of sexual problems can be attributed to one or more sources, which are not mutually exclusive and which often overlap

The causes of sexual problems in men vary, but generally they might be attributed to one or more of four sources: physiological, psychological, relational, and sociocultural. These sources are, of course, overlapping domains and therefore represent convenient rather than mutually exclusive classifications. That is, a distressful relationship between the man and his partner may affect his psychological well-being, which in turn may influence his physiological response. Conversely, a man with a clear medical etiology responsible for diminishing erectile function may lose self-confidence and begin to avoid sexual intimacy, a situation that typically impacts the dyadic relationship.

Factors that contribute to development of a sexual dysfunction may be different from those that contribute to its maintenance

The etiological factors identified herein represent *potential* causes for problems, or "risk factors," in that while they increase the likelihood of a sexual dysfunction, they do not determine it. Furthermore, the factors responsible for precipitating or predisposing a sexual problem may be quite different from those that eventually end up maintaining it. For example, failure to respond with an adequate erection due to stress or medication may result in anxiety and diminished self-confidence surrounding future sexual encounters, factors that may eventually come to maintain or even intensify the problem. Finally, there is a great deal of variation in how each of these sources (physiological, psychological, relational, and sociocultural) might affect any given individual, with clear etiologies for some dysfunctional states simply not fully elaborated. In a broader sense, however, it is often useful to conceptualize each man as having his own biopsychosocial vulnerabilities, such that the combination of factors resulting in sexual dysfunction for one man may be quite different from those for another man. In the following sections, a number of common risk, predisposing, and maintaining factors for male sexual dysfunction are discussed (see Table 3).

Pathophysiological-Based Risk Factors

Given the priming role of testosterone in sexual arousability in men, disruption of the hypothalamic-pituitary-gonadal (HPG) axis is likely to lead to

Table 3
Examples of Common Risk, Predisposing, and Maintaining Factors for Male Sexual Dysfunction Using a Biopsychosocial Approach

Dysfunction	Pathophysiological	Psychological/ behavioral	Relationship
Erectile dysfunction	Tobacco use Diabetes mellitus Cardiovascular disease/hypertension Urinary tract disease Pelvic/spinal injury or trauma Chronic neurological disease Endocrine axis disturbances Various medications	Stress/emotional Depression/anxiety Performance anxiety Psychiatric disturbances Body image Arousal disorders	Partner dysfunction Hostility/anger Partner attractiveness
Premature ejaculation	Chronic neurological disease Pelvic/spinal injury or trauma Various medications Urinary tract disease Thyroid disease	Anxiety (general or specific) Novel situations or partners	Partner dysfunction Hostility/anger Control/dominance
Retarded/ inhibited ejaculation	Thyroid disease Urinary tract disease Neuropathy Various medications, alcohol	Idiosyncratic masturbation Low arousal Anxiety	Partner attractiveness Partner dysfunction
Hypoactive sexual desire disorder	Androgen deficiency Dopaminergic disturbances Prolactin imbalance	Depression Psychiatric disturbances History of sexual abuse General life stressors	

Note. Adapted from "Sexual Health and Problems: Erectile Dysfunction, Premature Ejaculation, and Orgasmic Disorders," by D. L. Rowland, in J. Grant & M. Potenza (Eds.), *Textbook of Men's Mental Health* (pp. 171–204). Arlington, VA: American Psychiatric Association Press, 2007.

loss of libido and sexual interest. Such problems, however, tend to be fairly uncommon and are typically accompanied by a variety of other physical/physiological symptoms. Although men having low or absent gonadal function (i.e., hypogonadal) may show little interest in sex, they are not necessarily impotent and may obtain erections when presented with certain kinds of psychosexual stimuli (see Bancroft, 1989). In general, however, these men are less likely to seek out or attend to sexual stimulation and fulfillment because of their hormone deficiency. As might be expected, diseases that interfere with neural control over the HPG axis (e.g., dopamine deficiency in Parkinson's disease) or that result in high levels of prolactin may also interfere with sexual desire.

In some instances, a cascading effect may occur such that decreased sexual interest results in reduced arousal and inability to maintain an erection.

Any condition, disease, or drug that diminishes responsivity of the nervous, vascular, and smooth muscle (autonomic) systems has the potential to disrupt the "mechanics" of erection (Feldman, Goldstein, Hatzichristou, Krane, & McKinlay, 1994). Common risk factors for ED directly or indirectly compromise the process of smooth muscle relaxation (and arteriole dilation) necessary for penile engorgement. In addition, disruption of neural control due to neuropathy or chronic neurological diseases also accounts for erectile impairment. In some instances, the association between a specific condition (e.g., low levels of dehydroepiandrosterone [DHEA]) and ED has been documented, but the mechanism of action has not yet been clarified. Risk factors that impact erectile function may in some instances be additive, in that the greater the number of conditions present that affect the response system (e.g., smoking plus diabetes), the greater the probable impact on erectile function.

Unlike risk factors for ED, pathophysiological risk factors for ejaculatory disorders – premature and retarded/inhibited ejaculation – do not have easily identifiable common underlying pathways. Factors most often correlated with ejaculatory disorders, however, are procedures, diseases, or conditions that interfere with the neural integrity in the genito-pelvic region (see Section 1.6 Comorbidities).

Age and Medications

Inasmuch as aging serves as a proxy for a general increase in pathophysiological conditions, it is not surprising that men over 50 years are much more likely to report problems with erection (Feldman et al., 1994; Lewis et al., 2004). Although age may also impact ejaculatory function, the relationship between the two is not always straightforward. An increased prevalence of premature ejaculation (PE) seen in men 50 and older probably represents the development of coexisting erectile problems in those age groups; that is, the PE may develop in response (or be secondary) to age-related ED. The long-time supposition that rapid ejaculation is attenuated with age, although logically sound, has not been adequately tested in longitudinal studies, and therefore no firm conclusions can be drawn. On the other hand, given that penile sensitivity decreases substantially with age (Rowland, 1998), a tendency toward increased ejaculatory latencies with aging is not implausible and may account for the slight increase in the prevalence of IE in older men. Finally, as might be expected, various medications and recreational drugs may interfere with erectile and ejaculatory function, including many medications commonly used for depression, hypertension, and gastrointestinal disturbances. Comprehensive reviews of the impact of psychotropic agents on sexual function, many of which are used increasingly with age, are available (e.g., see Clayton & Balon, 2009).

> The relationship between age and ejaculatory function is not always straightforward

Psychological Risk Factors for Male Sexual Dysfunction

In contrast to the pathophysiological risk factors noted above, the relationships among psychological risk or predisposing factors and sexual dysfunction are substantially more tenuous (though no less important) and more likely to affect the entire sexual response cycle rather than just specific components. Also, because psychological factors are many and varied, they have the potential to interact with sexual response through a variety of processes. For example, a major psychiatric disorder – such as clinical depression or schizophrenia (DSM-IV, Axis 1 disorders) – is likely to affect sexual response in a different manner than, say, personality or developmental disorders (DSM IV, Axis 2). And these may differ substantially from the way in which a lack of self-confidence stemming from anxiety about performance impacts sexual response. This section reviews seven broad categories of psychological risk factors for sexual dysfunction. These categories include:

- evaluative factors,
- problems surrounding sexual arousal,
- general psychosocial stressors,
- developmental factors,
- personality profiles,
- major psychopathology,
- relationship factors.

Evaluative Factors

The overwhelming majority of erection problems – and perhaps premature ejaculation problems as well – that are psychological in nature, stem from the evaluative nature of sexual response (hence the common reference to sexual "performance"). Anxiety stemming from the man's lack of confidence to perform adequately, to appear and feel attractive (body image), to satisfy his partner sexually, to experience an overall sense of self-efficacy, and – despite New Age efforts to downplay the idea – to measure up against the competition is likely to impact most men at some point in their lives (Althof et al., 2004; Zilbergeld, 1993). This anxiety often generates a number of maladaptive responses, such as the man's setting unrealistic expectations or focusing attention on his own sexual response (i.e., self-monitoring) at the cost of attending to important erotic cues from the partner. Such problems often arise from various cultural expectations and stereotypes linked to the male gender role. Although these evaluative issues tend to surface at the beginning of a new relationship, they may also emerge when the ongoing balance in a relationship is changed or disrupted. These issues may be embedded in the relationship itself (and therefore might also be viewed as "relationship" risk factors), but they may also be the consequence of factors that impact the relationship in indirect ways. Thus, the man's loss of employment and his subsequent reduced self-esteem, a partner's extramarital relationship, or the introduction of a new family member into the household (child, elderly parent, etc.) are examples of factors that often change the ongoing sexual-dyadic relationship.

Cultural expectations and stereotypes related to the male gender role often play a role in evaluative factors that contribute to erection problems

Problems Surrounding Subjective Sexual Arousal

Perhaps more a symptom than an actual risk factor, subjective sexual arousal may play a role in some sexual dysfunctions. In men with erectile problems stemming from evaluative factors (such as those mentioned above), subjective arousal may be normal and high, but genital response may be diminished or absent. In contrast, men who report inhibited or delayed ejaculation often report lower levels of subjective arousal while showing strong erectile response. In a similar vein, men with premature ejaculation often report hyperarousability

Rapid onset to ejaculation may be related to any one of the multiple factors that drive subjective sexual arousal

during psychosexual stimulation, and recent findings do suggest that such men may underestimate their physiological/genital arousal (Rowland & Cooper, 2005). For these reasons, some argue that disorders of ejaculation may be more a problem of arousal than a problem with the ejaculatory process per se. Of course, since a man's sexual arousal level is driven by multiple factors, including sexual interest, partner stimulation and attraction, context, time since last ejaculation, anticipation, and so on, a rapid onset to ejaculation may be related to any of a number of possible psychological and relationship factors.

General Psychosocial Stressors

Significant life events that result in long-term or acute depression may also lead to sexual dysfunction. Populations of aging and diabetic men, for example, often show a higher incidence of depression and anxiety than younger or healthy counterparts; they are also more likely to exhibit low sexual desire and erectile difficulties (Harland & Huws, 1997; Schreiner-Engel & Schiavi, 1986; Tsitouras & Alvarez, 1984). However, unlike the relationship between "performance" anxiety and sexual dysfunction, the relationship between general psychosocial stressors and sexual dysfunction is less obvious. In addition, because nonpsychotic depression and anxiety are not easily separated from the pathophysiological effects of aging, illness, and stress, it is not clear which factors might be responsible for the sexual dysfunction: the pathophysiological condition itself or the associated psychological states of depression and anxiety. Perhaps it is safest to conclude that sexual dysfunction is compounded by depression and anxiety in these men (and the depression and anxiety themselves may produce physiological changes such as increased cortisol production) but not solely due to these psychological factors. Indeed, depression and anxiety associated with various life events may just as likely result from the sexual problems as cause them.

Developmental Factors

> Higher levels of depression and anxiety are found in men seeking help for sexual problems than in the general population

Early traumatic sexual experiences may also impair sexual responding. Although it is difficult to identify specific events and the process through which they operate, child sexual abuse has consistently been shown to affect adult sexual interest, and subsequently sexual arousal and erectile/ejaculatory function (Loeb et al., 2002). Perhaps just as frequently, however, child sexual abuse is manifested in maladaptive paraphilias and nonsexual behaviors (e.g., drug use, eating disorders, etc.). Other developmental issues may play important roles in sexual problems. For example, unresolved gender identity issues and restrictive sexual attitudes and/or practices in the family-of-origin household may predispose sexual dysfunction. The man's ability to overcome developmental traumas is often related to therapeutic intervention and/or his own level of resiliency.

Personality Profiles of Men with Sexual Dysfunction

> Dysfunctional men display a tendency toward greater self-consciousness and vulnerability and lower openness

A number of studies have attempted to profile the type of male personality prone to sexual dysfunction. Although results are mixed, the most consistent pattern to emerge is that men seeking help for sexual problems exhibit higher levels of depression and anxiety than sexually functional counterparts (Angst, 1998; Costa, Fagan, Piedmont, Ponticas, & Wise, 1992). In contrasting the different kinds of sexual dysfunction, one study (Tondo, Cantone, Carta, & Laddomada, 1991) suggests that men with erectile problems manifest their anxiety primarily through negative self-image and low self-esteem, whereas men with PE do so through symptoms more characteristic of hypomanic states such as agitation and mild obsession. The relationship between depression, anxiety, and sexual dysfunction appears to extend beyond erectile and ejaculatory disorders. For example, couples indicating low sexual interest (hypoactive sexual desire disorder) have a higher propensity for past or current chronic depression than might typically be expected, a finding that may mirror the low sex interest in depressed populations. Yet, when depression and anxiety are excluded from the picture, no single personality profile consistently characterizes men with sexual dysfunction, although several personality characteristics may be relevant. A tendency toward greater self-consciousness and vulnerability and lower openness seems most consistently to describe dysfunctional men, characteristics that may lead to diminished appreciation of varied experiences and act to sustain performance anxiety associated with male sexual dysfunction. Furthermore, men who score low in warmth may have difficulty with intimacy or commitment, suggesting a need for treatment focusing on establishing greater interpersonal intimacy.

Major Psychopathology

Chronic psychopathology has long been a suspected cause of sexual dysfunction. Both depression and schizophrenia are associated with diminished sexual desire, impairment of arousal, and loss or delay of ejaculation, and not surprisingly, sexual dysfunction occurs in a high percentage of depressed and schizophrenic patients (estimated from 35 to 75% [Baldwin, 1996; Lilleleht & Leiblum, 1993]). However, the extent to which the psychopathology actually causes the dysfunction is unclear, as few studies have documented sexual functioning prior to the onset of the mental illness or adequately separated the effects of antipsychotic treatment through medication (which itself may have antisexual effects) from those of the depression itself. Furthermore, the extent to which the effect on sexual response represents general malaise, social withdrawal, or inability to experience pleasure rather than a specific effect on a psychosexual process is undetermined. Although the definitive studies have yet to be done, the bulk of the research suggests that the primary effect on sexual dysfunction is mediated through diminished interest in sex, which in turn affects arousal/erectile and orgasmic response. Thus, for individuals manifesting major mental disorders, treatment typically focuses first on alleviating the psychological condition.

Relationship Factors

Relationship factors that affect sexual function are undoubtedly the most difficult to pinpoint and describe in brief catch-all phrases. Nevertheless, the lack of an adequate/appropriate nosology should not be misconstrued as a lack of importance. Indeed, many of the dysfunction precipitating and/or maintaining factors mentioned above involve a relationship component. Furthermore, because the quality of the sexual relationship often hinges on the overall quality of the marital/partner relationship, these two elements are highly interdependent (Althof et al., 2004; Schnarch, 2000).

Several specific relationship factors associated with male sexual dysfunction include partner dysfunctions, partner expectations and perceived evaluation of performance, and perceived attractiveness of the partner. Within the relationship itself, the progression from a novel, partner-focused style early in the relationship to a more routinized self-gratification style, concomitantly affected by the intrusion of work and family, is often cause for emotional issues that may in part be manifested through sexual dysfunction. Cognitive-emotional issues such as lack of intimacy and trust and general anger or hostility directed toward or perceived from the partner are likely to impact sexual interactions and response. Issues of relationship "control" and dominance also frequently emerge as mediating factors for sexual problems. As has been noted by clinicians for years, because sexual gratification is often in the control of the partner, the degree that such gratification is actively sought by one member of the dyad, the greater the control the other member exerts over that individual.

The quality of the sexual relationship is often related to the quality of the overall marital or partner relationship

Probably more important than any single relationship factor is the overall quality of the relationship itself. Specifically, any event, factor, or situation that interferes with passion, intimacy, commitment, or communication is likely to have a disruptive effect on the sexual relationship. Thus, preceding sex therapy with couples' therapy for those with significant relationship issues tends to result in better outcomes for the sex therapy, while couples therapy in nondistressed couples does not typically lead to improved sexual functioning (Carey, 1998; Rowland, Cooper, & Slob, 1998). Conversely, sex therapy in nondistressed couples often does lead to improved dyadic functioning.

1.5   Differential Diagnosis

Key starting point for evaluation and treatment frequently involves identifying outcomes and goals identified by the patient (and his partner)

In an era of pharmacotherapeutics, the field of sexology has gradually migrated from a primary emphasis on differential diagnosis (e.g., biogenic versus psychogenic origin) toward a model of client- or patient-centered treatment. In other words, because pharmaceuticals can produce positive end results no matter what the etiology of the problem (e.g., PDE-5 inhibitors such as Viagra work well on men with a variety of psychological or biological etiologies), the key starting point often involves identifying the outcomes and goals sought by the patient (and his partner). The clinician – whether physician or therapist – then develops a strategy that, in conjunction with the couple, moves the patient toward those goals.

Four dimensions – biological, psychological, relationship, and sociocultural – all have potential to contribute to sexual functional impairment

Such an approach does not obviate the value of a differential diagnosis, and understanding factors that contribute to the patient's impairment is critical to any diagnostic process and effective treatment. This approach does, however, acknowledge the fact that the tools available for the treatment of most sexual problems in men may represent a combination of strategies, some of which may not necessarily be directly related to the cause of the problem.

As discussed in Chapter 2, most dysfunctions are best viewed as involving multiple dimensions of the individual – the biological, psychological, relationship, and sociocultural. Since all such dimensions are rooted in some form of neurophysiological processing, it is probably most useful to view problems as occurring within a 4-dimensional grid, whereby each dimension has the potential to make a relative contribution to the functional impairment.

1.6   Comorbidities

Similar to other chronic conditions that occur in primary care patients, medical and psychiatric comorbidities are not uncommon in men with sexual dysfunctions. In fact, risk factors and comorbidities often overlap – what begins as a risk factor may eventually develop into a comorbid condition, and in some instances the two may represent different manifestations of a common underlying cause. Such is the case with erectile dysfunction and heart disease – ED may serve as a marker for cardiovascular problems, and conversely, cardiovascular problems (and medications) may guide the physician or clinician to query the patient about concurrent erectile problems.

Risk factors and comorbidities often overlap; what begins as a risk factor may develop into a comorbid condition

Low sexual desire has been associated with a multitude of conditions (Table 3, Hypoactive Sexual Desire). Perhaps most common is that of androgen deficiency and/or hypogonadism. The effects of low androgen, particularly testosterone, on sexual desire are likely direct, in that this hormone has consistently been shown to improve sexual desire in men with androgen deficiency (Hackett, 2008). But the effects may also be more subtle and less direct: Deficiency of androgen has been associated with depression and lethargy, conditions which themselves may attenuate sexual desire. Furthermore, testosterone may be metabolized to estradiol – a common estrogen – in both the gonads and peripheral tissue, and this hormone may act synergistically with testosterone in a positive manner on sexual drive.

Other endocrine conditions also correlate strongly with low sexual desire and, in some instances, with low testosterone. One such condition is hyperprolactinemia, a condition in which increased prolactin secretion (due to a tumor, certain medications, or even elevated estrogen) may interfere with sexual desire and erectile response. Elevated cortisol – an index of stress, adrenal dysregulation, or antidepressant use – has also been associated with low sexual desire.

There are many medical and/ or psychological conditions correlated with low sexual desire

Finally, a number of other medical or psychological conditions are correlated with loss of sexual interest, including cardiovascular disease, renal failure, epilepsy, depression, anxiety, emotional problems and stress, and relationship conflict. Daily alcohol consumption and fair-to-poor health are also predictors of low sexual desire. The mechanisms through which these conditions affect sexual desire are probably more general in nature – that is, such events often necessitate rearrangement of life's priorities and, in so doing, sexual interest takes a lower position on the hierarchy of needs.

Erectile dysfunction resulting from a pathophysiological condition is typically not a specific or isolated condition, but rather just one manifestation of an underlying disease process that affects neurovascular function (Lewis, Yuan, & Wang, 2008). Thus, ED is often seen in men with any number of chronic diseases that impair vascular function – whether the result of neuropathy that interferes with innervation of smooth neuromusculature of vascular tissue, or of the inability of the vascular smooth muscle to respond to innervation due

Any disease or injury that impairs neural or vascular response of the genital region is likely to affect erectile response

to, for example, the loss of the elasticity response of the vascular musculature. In short, any disease or injury that impairs neural or vascular response of the genital region is a likely comorbidity.

One of the most common coexisting conditions with ED is diabetes mellitus, a disease whose prevalence increases with age. But other conditions are common as well, including other metabolic disturbances (which may manifest in obesity); atherosclerosis (hypertension), which may result in arterial lesions; other cardiovascular problems such as hypercholesterolemia; chronic renal failure; and clinical depression. Treatment of these conditions may lead to partial or complete recovery of erectile response (as with renal transplants) although the medications used to treat these conditions may themselves interfere with erectile response. Indeed, in the patient with no cardiovascular symptoms, suspected biogenic ED is now considered a reason to investigate broader underlying cardiovascular disease.

Various genitourinary diseases such as those classified as lower urinary tract symptoms are also known to cause erectile failure. And, as expected, injury to any of the central (brain and spinal) neural pathways may cause and coexist with ED. Finally, due to the interdependence of the phases of sexual response, factors that affect sexual desire may also interfere with erection.

Premature ejaculation sometimes occurs with various other conditions, although a direct causal effect is less apparent. For example, PE often is prevalent (or overrepresented) in men with diabetes, chronic pelvic pain syndrome, thyroid disease, social phobia, anxiety/depression, and posttraumatic stress disorder (see Rowland, 2011). In addition, PE and ED often co-occur: Large population studies indicate that of those men reporting PE, 32% also reported problems with ED. Such reports suggest that the presence of PE should be considered in men with specific chronic medical illnesses, anxiety/depression, and ED.

> **The causes for PE and IE are not well understood**

Delayed and inhibited ejaculation (IE) may result from any disease or injury that disrupts the ejaculatory process. In some instances, a somatic condition may account for delayed or inhibited ejaculation, and indeed, any procedure or disease that disrupts sympathetic or somatic innervation to the genital region has the potential to affect ejaculatory function and orgasm. Thus, spinal cord injury, multiple sclerosis, pelvic-region surgery, severe diabetes, and medications that inhibit α-adrenergic innervation of the ejaculatory system have been associated with inhibited ejaculation (Masters & Johnson, 1966; Shafik, 1998). All types of delayed or inhibited ejaculation show age-related increases in prevalence and, independent of age, increased severity with lower urinary tract symptoms (Blanker et al., 2001; Motofei & Rowland, 2005a). Commonly used medications, particularly antidepressants, may delay ejaculation as well (see Perelman, McMahon, & Barada, 2004). Nevertheless, sizable numbers of men with delayed or inhibited ejaculation exhibit no clear somatic comorbidities that account for or occur with this disorder.

1.7   Diagnostic Procedures and Documentation

A number of validated instruments are available to assist in the diagnosis of sexual dysfunctions. However, even before administering standardized diagnostic tools, a preliminary "screening" is often useful to identify the nature of the problem and determine whether it falls within the traditional classifications of sexual dysfunction. The "screen" typically consists of a series of short questions (see the Appendix 3 for sample questions) that can also specify which phase or phases of the sexual response cycle are affected, and further, whether one problem might be secondary to another. For example, a man who has difficulty reaching ejaculation/orgasm may not reach sufficiently high levels of sexual arousal, and therefore the problem may lie not in the ejaculatory response per se, but rather in his level of arousal.

The diagnostic tools mentioned in this section represent only a sampling of some of those available. Furthermore, these assessments do not serve as substitutes for a traditional clinical interview and diagnosis. Rather, they help confirm that a problem exists and provide preliminary information that may, along with the results of the "screen," offer a segue into further discussion of the problem.

Such assessment tools provide a starting point for identifying and discussing a sexual problem, but they should not replace a clinical interview and diagnosis

1.7.1   International Index of Erectile Function (IIEF)

The International Index of Erectile Function (IIEF), introduced in 1997, is a self-report assessment of sexual functioning. The IIEF is best known for evaluation of sexual function in clinical trials, but because it consists of only 15 items, it can be used readily as a clinical tool. The 15 items are subdivided into five domains: erectile function, orgasmic function, sexual desire, intercourse satisfaction, and overall satisfaction (Rosen, Cappelleri, & Gendrano, 2002).

1.7.2   Sexual Health Inventory for Men (SHIM)

The Sexual Health Inventory for Men (SHIM) is also known as the IIEF-5 and actually represents an abridged version of the IIEF. Specifically, the five items dealing with erectile function drawn from the larger 15-item IIEF can be used as the basis for a preliminary office assessment once ED is suspected. The five questions of the SHIM evaluate the severity of male sexual dysfunction on 5-point scales, ranging from very low to very high, with questions about sexual confidence, firmness of erection, difficulty and frequency of maintaining an erection, and satisfaction (Rosen, Cappelleri, Smith, Lipsky, & Pena, 1999).

1.7.3   Self-Esteem and Relationship Questionnaire (SEAR)

The Self-Esteem and Relationship Questionnaire (SEAR) is designed to measure satisfaction within a relationship (Cappelleri et al., 2004). Included are sexual relationship and overall relationship satisfaction, as well as sexual confidence, especially for men with ED. Specifically, this 14-item questionnaire can be used to assess the impact of ED on relationship factors, including the man's self-esteem, confidence, and the satisfaction with the sexual relationship. The SEAR generates four subscale scores: sexual relationship satisfaction, confidence, self-esteem, and overall relationship satisfaction; when tallied, these subscales generate an overall score (Cappelleri et al., 2007).

1.7.4   Male Sexual Health Questionnaire (MSHQ)

The Male Sexual Health Questionnaire (MSHQ) is aimed at evaluation of sexual function and satisfaction in older men but may also be used with some effectiveness in men of varying ages. With 25 items, the MSHQ evaluates erection, ejaculation, and satisfaction. A focus on ejaculatory function adds significantly to this instrument, as not many assessment tools tap this aspect of sexual functioning. The MSHQ purportedly has greater cultural sensitivity than other tools (Rosen et al., 2004a).

1.7.5   Premature Ejaculation Prevalence and Attitudes (PEPA)

The Premature Ejaculation Prevalence and Attitudes (PEPA) survey was developed for studies examining the prevalence of PE, comorbidities, PE-related behaviors and attitudes, and professional help seeking (Porst et al., 2007). Several key questions address concepts of ejaculation used to classify men as having PE, including low or absent control over ejaculation and whether this condition is viewed as a problem by the man and/or his partner.

1.7.6   Index of Premature Ejaculation (IPE)

The Index of Premature Ejaculation (IPE) is a 10-item questionnaire designed for the assessment of control over ejaculation, satisfaction with sex life, and distress in men with PE (Althof et al., 2006). The IPE was developed to measure subjective aspects of premature ejaculation, other than ejaculatory latency, and has the potential to add value to the evaluation of the treatment of PE.

1.7.7   Premature Ejaculation Diagnostic Tool (PEDT)

The Premature Ejaculation Diagnostic Tool (PEDT) is a five-item tool used for diagnosing premature ejaculation using DSM-IV-TR criteria regarding PE. The five items assess such dimensions as control, frequency, minimal sexual stimulation, distress, and interpersonal difficulty. This tool is meant to help clinicians without much experience in diagnosing PE. It is easy to use, with a simple format to provide a fast and reliable way to assess complaints (Symonds et al., 2007a; Symonds et al., 2007b).

1.7.8   Quality of Erection Questionnaire (QEQ)

The Quality of Erection Questionnaire (QEQ) was developed as a means for patients concerned with their erectile function, to evaluate their levels of satisfaction with erection quality. The QEQ consists of six items evaluating the hardness of an erection, time to hardness and length of erection, and overall quality. The questionnaire is based on the knowledge that hardness is a key factor in determining overall satisfaction with an erection. It allows for the needs perceived by the patient to be evaluated in parallel with treatment of ED (Porst et al., 2007).

1.7.9   Sexual Quality of Life Measure for Men (SQOL-M)

The Sexual Quality of Life Measure for Men (SQOL-M) is an 11-item questionnaire that assesses the quality of life in men suffering from ED, who in clinical situations often report lower quality of life associated with this problem. The questionnaire can be completed in about 5 minutes by males 18 years of age and older (Abraham, Symonds, & Morris, 2008).

2

Theories and Models of Sexual Dysfunction

2.1   Introduction and Issues

Models of sexual response may have different approaches or focus on different factors of sexual responding, but all models have limitations

There are any number of ways of thinking about and modeling sexual response. For example, a model may take a descriptive physiological approach, as characterized by Masters and Johnson's (1966) sexual response cycle of general/ genital arousal, plateau, and orgasm. It may focus on factors that contribute to sexual responding (e.g., the general biopsychosocial model: Engel, 1977). It may address primarily the cause of sexual *problems* (e.g., Kaplan's [1974, 1979] inclusion of "desire," Perelman's "tipping point" model [Perelman & Rowland, 2006]). It may analyze sexual response into various components for the purpose of generating research hypotheses and explaining the occurrence of sexual behavior (Bancroft, Graham, Janssen, & Sanders, 2009). Finally, it may view sexual behavior as simply one component in the much larger picture of the person's overall sexuality that includes attitudes, gender identity, sexual orientation, sexual behavior, and so on.

All models naturally have liabilities. They focus on specific elements of the sexual response at the expense of omitting others; they may be so all-encompassing as to provide little useful direction to the practitioner wanting a simplified working model for application; they may be outdated as new research uncovers previously unknown relationships; or they may perpetuate ways of thinking that are inadequate or inaccurate (e.g., see Basson's 2001 model that provides an alternative perspective on women's sexual desire).

Several points about models of sexual function are worth noting:

- Theories and models are generated to help researchers and clinicians think about and understand sexual behavior and response, but no one particular theory or model will serve as the *best* conceptualization of sexual response for all situations and purposes.

Models used by clinicians are seldom meaningful to patients

- Models seldom have meaning for patients or clients, as their experience of sexual response is usually simple and undifferentiated. For example, they do not think of orgasm/ejaculation as being a separate process from arousal and erection. Indeed, these differentiations are simply convenient distinctions that help clinicians focus in on various parts of sexual response and dysfunction.

Models often dichotomize men into functional and dysfunctional categories rather than recognize the problem as a continuum

- Approaches, models, and definitions that focus on sexual dysfunction often dichotomize people into functional and dysfunctional groups whereas in reality, function–dysfunction lies along a continuum. The dichotomization process may serve the needs of medicine and medical reimbursement, but it may not necessarily best serve the needs of the patient and/or clinician.

2.2   Modified Biopsychosocial Model

One easy and effective way for clinicians to approach sexual dysfunction in men is to consider possible risk and etiological factors from an "expanded" biopsychosocial model (see Figure 1, Table 3). The relevant domains of this investigatory model include:
- biological/physiological factors,
- psychological factors,
- relationship factors,
- sociocultural factors.

2.2.1   Biological/Physiological Factors

These factors include primarily those that are pathophysiological or iatrogenic. As mentioned previously, acute or chronic diseases, injury, and surgical procedures (e.g., prostatectomy) that compromise neural or vascular function particularly in the pelvic region are potential contributors to, or causes of, sexual functioning. Medications may also affect all phases of sexual functioning – sexual interest, erectile function, and ejaculatory function – either individually or in combination. In some instances, natural biological variation may also play a role, although its effects are less clear: For example, the latency to ejaculation can be described as a positively skewed distribution (see Figure 2), with some men experiencing very short latencies for all of their sexual lives and others experiencing very long latencies.

Pathophysiology rather than natural biological variation plays the more prominent role in sexual dysfunction

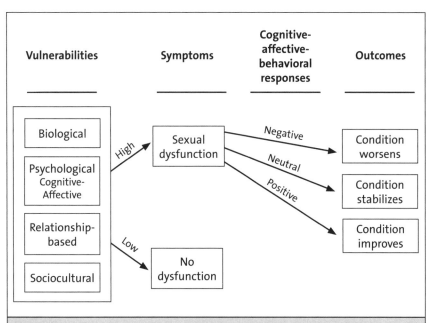

Figure 1
Conceptualizing sexual response and the diagnosis and treatment of sexual dysfunction through an expanded biopsychosocial model.

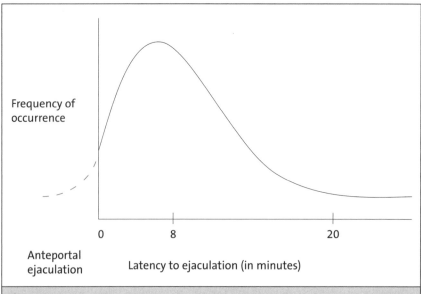

Figure 2
Positively skewed distribution for latency to ejaculation (in minutes) beginning from the moment of insertion. Anteportal ejaculation occurs prior to the time of insertion.

2.2.2   Psychological Factors

Psychological factors often overlap with biological factors; for example, the psychological condition of "anxiety" is often manifested in somatic changes. Psychological factors encompass all those elements comprising the person's psychological past and present that ultimately underlie his attitudes, beliefs, values, expectations, attributions, cognitions, thoughts, emotions, and behaviors (see Rowland & Cooper, 2011). These processes may be affected by inherent dispositions having a biological/genetic basis, developmental-learning experiences which vary among individual men, or sociocultural environments that not only vary across but also within cultures, countries, peoples, and nations. Additionally, psychological factors may be enduring and trait-like (suggesting an underlying personality characteristic), or they may be transient and state-like (suggesting a response to a specific situation or crisis). Finally, the psychological processes may be occurring within a relatively normal range (e.g., a man who is *upset* or bothered by his condition of rapid ejaculation) or they may extend beyond the normal range such that they become "clinically significant" (e.g., a man who becomes *obsessed* with his condition to the point where it affects relationships, work, sense of well-being, etc.).

> **Psychological processes may be affected by inherent dispositions, developmental-learning experiences, or sociocultural environments**

2.2.3   Relationship Factors

Such factors generally overlap with psychological factors, but they are often complex and develop – sometimes imperceptibly – over time. For example, psychological distress may arise from specific dynamics occurring within the dyadic relationship. Both ED and PE involve complex relational processes, including increasingly intense sequences of partner-to-partner reactivity that often follow and serve to maintain or exacerbate the problem (Osborne & Rowland, 2007). In other words, psychological and relational processes not only impact the formation and course of the problem, the sexual problem itself has the potential to impact the physiological, psychological, and relational functioning of the individual and his partner. As an example, it is not uncommon for a female partner to develop hypoactive desire in response to the man's ejaculatory difficulties. The partner may "personalize" the man's premature ejaculation, convincing herself that his problem is a direct reflection of some inadequacy of her own or his selfish failure to consider her needs. The relational tension that emerges in such scenarios is further exacerbated when the male becomes even more severely symptomatic, perhaps developing comorbid erectile difficulties in response to his partner's disappointment. In such a scenario, a clear understanding of the man's sexual dysfunction requires attention to the complex interplay among these physiological, psychological, and relationship processes.

There is a complex interrelatedness between relationship factors, psychological factors, and physiological processes

2.2.4   Sociocultural Factors

Sociocultural factors are typically derived from a person's perceived role in society, particularly with respect to gender roles. For this reason, they affect both the man's relationship with the partner and his own psychological functioning, as they set up expectations for him and his partner which may or may not be met, or even realistic. Although such expectations have always been relevant to sexual response, it is only recently, as Western society has become not just more multicultural but more sensitive to multicultural issues, that these factors become salient within the context of the diagnosis of sexual problems and their subsequent treatment. Thus, specific cultures may place greater or lesser emphasis on having multiple partners, on monogamy, on male-centric pleasure, on equality of partners, on performance issues related to endurance, and so on. Such values and expectations contribute to the man's self-perceptions, experiences, and self-definition of adequate sexual performance, and clearly impact his relationship with his partner.

The expectations for a man and partner are influenced by sociocultural factors, which contribute to his self-perception and self-definition of sexual performance

Often tied to cultural influence, religion may also play an important role in men's attitudes toward sex. For example, the defined purpose for sex (e.g., procreation) may place restrictions on nonprocreative sexual activities or may define specific conditions and times during which coital activity is permitted. Religious scripture may also define appropriate roles and sanctions for men and women within the sexual/marital relationship – for example, placing value on women's virginity or submissiveness of wives – which then may become embedded in the legal code of the culture or country. In many parts of the world, forcible sex within a marital relationship or with child brides is considered assault or rape and therefore illegal; in other parts of the world, such action is condoned as socially appropriate.

2.2.5   Interaction of the Biopsychosocial Domains

Sexual dysfunctions operate in much the same way as most other clinical problems

The four domains in the expanded biopsychosocial model are not distinct and independent categories – they overlap and interact, and they are dynamic and changing (Table 3). Assuming this perspective, there is every reason to believe that sexual dysfunction operates in much the same way as most other clinical problems: Specifically, an individual's biopsychosocial vulnerability interacts with specific developmental and current experiences and manifests as a specific disorder (Ragin, 2011) – in this case, sexual dysfunctional symptomatology. The particular biological, psychological, relationship, and social vulnerabilities related to developing, maintaining, or exacerbating the sexual dysfunction – as well as their relative balance – are idiosyncratic. Yet a *general* tendency toward vulnerability may be characteristic of specific subgroups, such as men who are predisposed toward specific chronic diseases, toward anxiety responding, toward perfectionistic performance expectations, toward partners who are highly critical, etc. (Rowland & Cooper, 2011).

An individual's response pattern to performance failures can influence the development of sexual problems

Furthermore, the individual's pattern of responding to performance failures also has a significant influence on functioning within these various domains, and this, in turn, influences the development of sexual problems. For example, attributions of external reasons for sexual impairment – such as consuming too much alcohol – are less likely to lead to anticipatory anxiety than internal attributions such as interpretations of loss of endurance and thus manliness, or of an age-related and inevitable functional loss (Fichten, Spector, & Libman, 1988). As a further example, those having a low tolerance for risk may be more likely to avoid sexual encounters and, when these do occur, to experience feelings of pressure and monitoring of performance – both of which are counterproductive to functional sexual response. The challenge is in understanding the relative etiological contribution to the sexual problem from each of the domains and, further, to determine which factors are primary, secondary, tertiary, and so on.

3

Diagnosis and Treatment Indications

Ideally, evaluation of a sexual problem involves an in-depth analysis of the specific problem, its severity, etiology, and contributing/maintaining factors. In practice, evaluation procedures vary widely, depending on the door through which the man enters the health system when seeking help. In the primary care physician's office, where economic factors (e.g., third-party reimbursement) may restrict the investment of time, and where lack of expertise about non-medical factors involved in sexual problems may limit the scope of the conversation, the evaluation may be cursory and superficial. In contrast, psychiatrists and behavioral/mental health clinicians, whose qualifications increase the likelihood for third-party reimbursement for delving into psychological and interpersonal issues, may undertake a thorough evaluation that extends through one or more sessions. Such evaluations typically include a complete medical and psychological history, the use of standardized assessment instruments, and a psychosexual history that includes the man's sexual partner.

Evaluation of a sexual problem will depend on where and from whom an individual seeks help

3.1 Establishing a General Framework for Evaluation

The *patient-directed* approach to the treatment of sexual disorders has recently gained popularity within the clinical/medical community. In this approach, primary consideration is given to the specific therapeutic goals and preferences of the patient, making it one of the clinician's main tasks to identify the most appropriate means to achieve those goals. In such instances, diagnostic procedures may be limited, because etiology may not necessarily guide the type of treatment eventually selected. Usually, however, some minimal attempt is made to identify potential medical disorders that might interfere with sexual functioning. Furthermore, since patient-centered therapy focuses on a holistic approach that views patient satisfaction – rather than just resolution of the symptoms – as one of the primary outcomes of treatment, at least some exploration of psychological, relationship, and sociocultural issues is likely to be carried out to avoid misdirected treatment. This process is consistent with the idea that the more the provider understands about potential factors responsible for the etiology and maintenance of the dysfunction, the wider the range of treatment options available, and therefore the more the treatment can be tailored to the specific needs of the individual. No matter what approach is taken, it is critical that the clinician works together with the patient (and his partner) in developing the treatment plan (Osborne & Rowland, 2007).

Exploration of the various issues responsible for the etiology and maintenance of the dysfunction provides for a wider range of treatment options

3.2   Organization of the Evaluation

Reduced to its simplest elements, a sexual assessment should identify:
(1) the nature and severity of the sexual dysfunction;
(2) medical/biological, psychological, relationship, and sociocultural factors that cause or contribute to the problem or that might diminish the effects of any particular treatment strategy;
(3) the needs and preferences of the patient and partner regarding treatment options.

The means by which each of these is achieved – through face-to-face interview, physical examination, symptom assessment scales, laboratory tests, or some combination thereof – may be driven by a number of factors, such as the specific orientation of the health provider and the resources and time available to the patient. For the behavioral or mental health clinician who encounters a man with sexual dysfunction, the assessment process should entail referral to a physician for a physical examination who then might determine whether further referral to a medical specialist (urologist, endocrinologist) is warranted or beneficial. On the other side, to optimize outcomes, medical specialists should refer any patient with a sexual dysfunction who enters the health care system through the "medical" door to a therapist for at least a brief assessment of general psychological, sociocultural, and relationship functioning.

> **Assessment of sexual dysfunction by behavioral or mental health clinicians should include referral to a physician for a physical examination**

3.3   Identifying the Problem and Quantifying Severity

The first step in the process requires identifying the specific problem – whether it is hypoactive sexual desire, erectile and arousal difficulty, premature ejaculation, inhibited orgasm/ejaculation, or some combination of these. Carefully worded questions related to each of these domains (see Appendix 3) are usually effective as an initial *screen* that helps establish where the specific problem lies. Optimally, each domain question should be augmented with further questioning to affirm the presence and type of the dysfunction.

Once the problem is identified, it is important to quantify its severity – for example, the frequency of occurrence of the dysfunctional response and the degree to which the response is impaired. For ED, such quantification may include an estimate of rigidity and/or the rate of successful coital attempts. For PE, parameters such as the estimated latency to ejaculation following vaginal penetration and the ability to delay (or control) ejaculation provide measures of impairment. For inhibited ejaculation, the ratio of orgasmic to coital episodes, estimated latency to orgasm, and general feelings of subjective arousal during coitus (e.g., relative to masturbation) offer a rudimentary index of severity. For all dysfunctions, the level of distress, bother, or dissatisfaction regarding sexual response and function is important to assess. A number of standardized assessment tools are available to assist clinicians with these tasks (see Section 1.7), but just as often a frank, focused, and progressive conversation regarding each of these components of the sexual response cycle will suffice.

> **Quantifying the sexual problem includes measures such as frequency of occurrence, the degree of impairment, and the level of distress**

3.4   Identifying Etiological Factors

The second step of the evaluation process typically accounts for most of the differences in approach among clinicians and health care providers. No matter how extensive or limited this step of the process might be, because sexual dysfunction may sometimes serve as a marker for other health problems (e.g., ED may signal cardiovascular disease, ejaculatory disorders may suggest prostate problems, and so forth), a physical examination is almost always warranted.

The primary care physician may well end the evaluative process at this point and simply move on to discussion of treatment options. In contrast, health care specialists (e.g., counselors, sex therapists) are likely to carry out further evaluation in the biological, psychological, relationship, and sociocultural domains, with bias toward those domains consistent with their clinical training. Although the traditional need to differentiate psychogenic from biogenic etiologies has become less critical with the introduction of effective biomedical interventions (that can alleviate specific dysfunctions of any origin), knowing whether the problem has strong psychological, relationship, or sociocultural components may assist any specialist in determining the most effective treatment therapy.

The need to differentiate psychogenic from biogenic etiologies is not as critical as it once was, but evaluation of relevant domains is helpful in determining effective treatment

3.4.1   Biomedical Assessment and Medical History

Medical assessments may be limited, moderate, or extensive. In addition to the physical examination, a family/medical history (regarding both acute and chronic diseases), including the use of prescription and over-the-counter medications, nutritional supplements, and recreational substances (tobacco, alcohol, cocaine, etc.), is typical. Beyond this, however, no broad consensus exists regarding what procedures are likely to yield information most helpful to the treatment process. Clearly, for men exhibiting hypoactive sexual desire disorder, a basic endocrine analysis for testosterone and prolactin is indicated. For men with ED, laboratory tests for comorbidities (e.g., diabetes mellitus, hyperlipidemia) and psychiatric assessment for mood disorders can help determine whether the dysfunction is secondary to another disease or condition. More extensive evaluations assessing vascular problems, autonomic functioning, sleep-related erections, or complete pituitary, gonadal, and adrenal hormone profiles are implemented less frequently (Rosen et al., 2004b). For ejaculatory disorders (premature and inhibited), no specific or reliable biomedical assessments are available that might shed further light on the problem beyond the information already obtained through the medical history (e.g., pelvic trauma or neuropathy) and basic physical examination.

There is no consensus about which specific medical assessments are likely to yield the best information useful for determining treatment

3.4.2   Psychosexual and Psychological Histories

In men, sexual functioning and psychological health are often interrelated. Indeed the two are bidirectional in nature, in that each has the potential to affect the other. In carrying out a psychosexual and general psychological evaluation, the clinician is better able to understand whether psychological (and relationship) factors contribute to sexual dysfunction and also whether they sustain or exacerbate the dysfunction. Whether considering cause or effect or the mutual and reciprocal flow between the two, one of the immediate goals of psychological evaluation is to determine which factors might be primary and which might be secondary, and thus where treatment should be focused.

At the individual psychological level, besides assessment for major or minor psychological disorders (depression, anxiety), the psychosexual history is perhaps the most critical element of the overall assessment process. The sexual history may be taken verbally, may make use of a script, and/or may involve any number of standardized assessment instruments available for this process (see Rosen et al., 2004b). In general, however, the evaluation may include information about:

The psychosexual history is a critical element in the assessment process

- Current and past sexual functioning;
- History (onset and duration) and specificity of the problem (e.g., with a particular partner; only during coitus and not during masturbation, etc.);
- Patient's understanding of and education about the problem;
- Patient's experience of the problem, including psychosocial factors surrounding the problem (fear of failure, etc.);
- Specific cultural expectations (see Section 3.4.4);
- Child and adolescent sexual histories and experiences when reason exists, such as suspected abuse;
- Family-of-origin attitudes and practices that might reveal important factors related to the sexual problem that will suggest specific treatment strategies.

Clinicians, of course, need to tread lightly when dealing with private and sensitive matters related to sexuality and should take steps to ensure that the patient does not feel stigmatized, judged, or embarrassed.

3.4.3   Relationship Assessment

A thorough understanding of a man's sexual response must include attention to relationship functioning

Because most sex is relational, the potential for a relationship contribution nearly always warrants investigation. From a theoretical perspective, the man's response *to* his partner and the response *of* his partner introduce potential factors that can explain much of the variance in sexual response (Osborne & Rowland, 2007). Thus a comprehensive understanding of the man's sexual response is not possible without some attention to the systemic (relationship) functioning of the couple. Such an approach also counters the bias in the sexual dysfunction field toward an exclusive individual etiology.

Thus, a relationship history that includes major events such as extramarital activity, divorce, separation, pregnancies (and related events such as miscarriages and abortions), and deaths should be noted, and any current relationship concerns or distress should be discussed (see Pridal & LoPiccolo, 2000). Standardized assessment instruments such as the Dyadic Adjustment Scale (DAS; Spanier, 1976) and Golombok Rust Inventory of Sexual Satisfaction (GRISS; Rust & Golombok, 1986) may be helpful in drawing out such concerns, as patients may be reluctant to appear critical of their partner's sexual, emotional, and behavioral interactions. Initially, the patient and partner may be assessed separately to avoid attributions of fault or blame, to identify potential partner dysfunctions and counterproductive attitudes, and to obtain each person's individual perspective (including distress) about the problem and its severity.

Finally, a sexually dysfunctional partner represents a potential source of a sexual problem for men. For example, a partner indicating a sexual aversion, low interest in or desire for sex, or anorgasmia may lead to difficulty with erection or even premature ejaculation so as to terminate intercourse quickly. More subtle dynamics within the relationship may also play an important role: A common consequence of sexual difficulty is frustration, which may lead to suppressed sexual interest on the man's part and subsequent diminished intimacy with the partner. In turn, these may affect a variety of other relationship dynamics. Withdrawal of sexual and emotional intimacy and lack of communication by one partner may lead to bewilderment, reduced trust, and feelings of diminished attractivity by the other partner. Further withdrawal by the partner along with discontent and anger may alter the relationship in such a way that treatment focused exclusively on genital response is neither effective nor relevant. In other words, the psychological and relational *causes and consequences* of the sexual problem may effectively neutralize most of the benefits received from improvement in genital response since such relationship dynamics are not readily reversed by attending solely to the genital problem (Conte, 1986; Corty, Althof, & Kurit, 1996).

3.4.4   Probing Sociocultural Factors

Men from different religious traditions and cultures view their sexuality very differently, and this view affects their performance, the perception of their performance, the perception of their partners, and so on. As a result, cultural and religious expectations – and specifically the extent to which the man perceives himself to be aligned with them – are likely to affect the sexual and power dynamics within a relationship. Thus, men may develop unrealistic expectations regarding initiation of sexual activity, duration of intercourse, assumptions regarding the partner's sexual enjoyment as well as who is responsible for it, and so on. Given that few individuals actually live up to the physical, sexual, and psychological stereotypes imbued by a culture, the potential for perceived failure, consequent negative thoughts and affects, and behavioral anomalies is significant. These cognitive-affective-behavioral patterns typically become well entrenched within the larger partner/sexual relationship and may be included as part of a broader discussion regarding cultural expectations.

> **Cultural and religious expectations can affect sexual and power dynamics within a relationship**

3.5   Defining the Desired Outcome

In the transition between evaluation and treatment, an important step lies in defining the relevant outcomes. Although the patient's and partner's involvement is essential to this process, men sometimes focus heavily on genital issues at the cost of neglecting more subtle, but no less important, psychological and interpersonal issues. Although clinicians would agree that treatment of the physical symptoms is crucial (e.g., prolongation of ejaculation latency, obtaining an erection sufficient for intercourse, etc.), most would also note that improved "genital performance" in the absence of improved sexual satisfaction and a better sexual relationship is meaningless (Rowland & Burnett, 2000). These latter outcomes, though not always easily quantified, typically correlate well with the overall measure of patient satisfaction with treatment (Hawton, 1998).

The outcomes of improved genital response, sexual satisfaction, and sexual relationship are interrelated, but may need to be addressed individually

Although these three outcomes – improved genital response, increased sexual satisfaction, and improved sexual relationship – are themselves interrelated, each may need to be addressed individually in the course of the therapeutic process. That is, in many situations, alleviation of the physical problem may improve the man's sexual satisfaction and the overall sexual relationship. But in others, the change in interpersonal dynamics that results from the dysfunction (e.g., avoidance of intimacy, or a partner's anger and distress) may not easily be reversed by merely "fixing" the genital dysfunction. In such cases, a number of psychological and interpersonal issues may need to be addressed, at least if increased sexual satisfaction and an improved sexual relationship are viewed as important outcomes.

3.6   Treatment of Male Sexual Dysfunction: Setting the Context

The clinician should have a thorough understanding of the patient's problem before beginning treatment

As mentioned in the previous section, before commencing treatment, the clinician should understand (1) the specific sexual problem, (2) the severity of the problem and the degree of functional impairment it causes, (3) at least broadly, if not in detail, the biological, psychological, relationship, and sociocultural factors that contribute to or maintain the problem, and (4) the specific treatment goals of the man and his partner. This understanding may be accomplished within a single session, or depending on the complexity of the problem, may require in-depth exploration over several sessions. These four elements converge to suggest an appropriate strategy that may utilize one, some, or all of the therapeutic tools available to the health care provider. Thus, oral medications and other biomedical treatments, bibliotherapy, individual sex therapy and counseling, and couples marital and/or sex therapy represent a range of options that may eventually constitute an effective treatment plan. Important to this approach, however, is not only the notion that each strategy can address a specific dimension of the problem, but that even when the etiology lies primarily within one domain (e.g., psychological anxiety), the use of auxiliary strategies (e.g., oral medications) may be helpful in achieving the larger goals of the patient and his partner. Finally, it is important for both clinician and patient to recognize early in the therapeutic process, the importance of and need for periodic follow-ups.

In the following section, general strategies available for the treatment of each of the four major male sexual dysfunctions – low sexual desire (hypoactive sexual desire disorder [HSDD]) or interest, erectile dysfunction (ED), premature ejaculation (PE), and delayed or inhibited ejaculation (IE) – are discussed.

4

Treatment

4.1 Treatment of Low Sexual Desire

4.1.1 Nomenclature and Definition

Low sexual desire has been recognized as a sexual problem for years, but was given heightened attention by Kaplan's conceptualization of sexual dysfunction in which desire played a key role (Kaplan, 1979). Clinically, the problem is referred to as hypoactive sexual desire disorder (HSDD), but colloquially the terminologies *loss of libido, low sexual desire,* or *low sexual interest* have been used interchangeably with each other and with HSDD. In some sexological circles, a distinction is made between *low sexual desire* and *low sexual interest,* the former referring primarily to conditions involving a biogenic origin, and the latter being a more encompassing term referring to either or both biogenic and psychogenic etiologies. For this discussion, issues regarding "desire" and "interest" are approached from the broadest possible perspective.

In terms of diagnosis, characteristics of low sexual desire include:

- Diminished or absent desire or interest, as operationalized partly through:
  - lack of sexual thoughts and fantasies,
  - lack of desire for sexual activity,
  - lack of responsiveness to sexual stimulation,
  - low frequency of sexual contact or initiation of sexual activity,
- Patient or partner concern about the condition.

Several comments and qualifications about low sexual desire are necessary, as the concept of desire itself is a slippery one.

(1) Unlike erection and ejaculation, sexual desire is not directly observable – that is, its presence (or absence) must be inferred through indirect measures. Indeed, sexual desire is a *construct* – an unobservable concept or variable presumed to be real but that cannot be measured directly – used to explain the frequency and intensity of behavior. Specifically, desire explains the frequency of occurrence of sexual behavior/response: Those with greater desire presumably have higher levels of sexual responsivity and response, and so on.

(2) Clinicians and researchers may fall into the trap of circular reasoning with such constructs: The construct itself is used to explain variation in the frequency and intensity of the behavior, but a conceptual problem arises when differences in the frequency and intensity of a behavior are then used to explain differences in sexual desire.

Sexual desire is a *construct* which cannot be measured directly

(3) Sexual desire is interrelated with the two other components of the sexual response cycle, erection/arousal and ejaculation. Men with low sexual desire may also suffer from low subjective sexual arousal, diminished erection, and delayed ejaculation. However, sexual desire may be negatively affected by problems with erection and ejaculation – the man may lose interest in his partner due to sexual inadequacy and embarrassment, and eventually avoid intimacy altogether.

(4) Clinicians and researchers have not clearly distinguished between low sexual desire that is inherently physiological and therefore primary, and that which is related to other psychological and relationship problems, and is therefore secondary.

4.1.2   Prevalence

The prevalence of low sexual desire is difficult to discern for several reasons.

- Men with low sexual desire, particularly those who are aging or suffering from disease, may not see the condition as a problem and therefore may have little motivation to seek treatment.
- Sexual desire exists along a continuum extending from high to low, so no specific cutoff threshold of desire can be invoked as an indicator of a dysfunction.
- To some extent, an appropriate level of sexual desire should be seen as a couples' issue; for example, a problem may be manifested when the couples are mismatched with respect to this level, or when the level of desire leads to other outcomes such as loss of interest in intimacy.

Men seldom focus on the lack of sexual desire as the issue that leads them to seek treatment

- Men seldom focus on issues of sexual desire; more often they are concerned with their erections and ejaculation. Even though these latter processes may be the direct consequence of low desire, men usually do not interpret the situation in this way and as a result may misinterpret their problem when participating in national surveys.

Estimates of prevalence, therefore, must be taken only as fairly crude guesses. Nevertheless, it appears that low sexual desire probably occurs in about 15–25% of men (Lewis et al., 2010). The challenge, of course, is that low sexual desire coexists with numerous other psychological and physical health problems and thus may wax and wane with these other conditions.

4.1.3   Risk Factors, Comorbidities, and Other Red Flags

Sexual desire does not just arise from endogenous factors such as hormones, but depends on many external factors

There are many sources of sexual desire (see Summary Box for factors that interfere with these sources). Classically, sexual desire in men is thought of as being "spontaneous" and "unprompted," that is, generally arising from within (endogenous), potentially ever present, and not stimulus-bound (perhaps best characterized by Freud's concept of libido or sexual energy, or similar to the construct of "hunger" with respect to food). In reality, sexual desire (and "interest") varies with many external factors, including context, partner, stimulation, and so on. For example, newly formed relationships are often more "sexually charged" than relationships that have stabilized over a period of time. In fact, in recent models of sexual response, sexual desire and sexual arousal are viewed more as synergistic and reciprocating processes (e.g., Basson, 2001) than distinct linear processes where desire → arousal → orgasm.

Sexual drive, as powerful as it may be at times, exists within a larger hierarchy of needs. Many of these needs can take precedence over sex – for example, hunger, thirst, sleep, and so on. Furthermore, conditions such as anxiety, depression, and other emotional states (e.g., anger) often lead to rearrangement of life priorities. In general, then, physical and psychological stressors may suppress sexual desire, as these stimulus conditions represent a necessity to attend to other needs.

For the sake of expediency, issues surrounding sexual desire have been conceptualized around three potential sources, as shown in the Summary Box:

Common Risk Factors for Low Sexual Desire and Interest

Endocrine and Neurochemical Factors
  Low levels of testosterone
  Older age (over 50 years)
  Hypogonadal functioning
  High levels of prolactin
  Unusually high estrogen or progesterone levels
  Other endocrine imbalances
  Neural-modulating medications (e.g., antidepressants, antiepileptics)

General Life Stressors
  Chronic/acute diseases effecting normal life function
  Psychobehavioral problems (depression, stress)

Relationship and Partner Issues
  Relationship changes
  Performance evaluation, expectations, and satisfaction of partner
  Personal characteristics and/or attributes of partner
  Partner dysfunction

Endocrine and Neurochemical Factors

Endocrine and neurochemical factors are interrelated, as endocrine factors affect sexual drive through their action on neurochemical systems in the brain (Gooren, 2008; Hackett, 2008). The most consistent relationship between sexual drive and hormones is androgen-based, particularly testosterone. Thus, men who are elderly (testosterone gradually declines with age) or men with hypogonadal functioning are prime candidates for low sexual desire. However, large intersubject variability regarding such relationships is common (Davidson, Kwan, & Greenleaf, 1982; Everitt, 1995). Typically, *minimal* morning levels of testosterone critical for normal sexual function hover around 6–9 nmol/L, but normal levels are usually around 10–12 nmol/L and such levels exceed those needed for normal functioning. However, the important factor is not just the overall level of circulating hormones, but the availability of the hormone to exert biological action on other systems. This "free" testosterone (that is, testosterone that is "not bound" to sex hormone binding globulin

Important to low sexual desire is not just the level of circulating testosterone, but its bioavailability to exert action on other systems

[SHBG] and therefore inactive) is a typical second assessment carried out in men with suspected low testosterone levels. Generally, if free testosterone is above about 2–3 nmol/L, then the man is not considered "androgen deficient." Men with more severe hypogonadal function typically show a range of other symptoms, including lethargy, decline in muscle mass, increase in fat mass, and a decrease in bone mineral density (Gooren, 2008). Since testosterone gradually declines with age, men over 50 years of age are at greatest risk for hypogonadal-induced low sexual desire.

Other hormones also have the potential to affect sexual desire in men. Because all gonadal hormones begin with the cholesterol molecule and follow fairly common pathways within the gonads – with levels of particular hormones dependent on the higher or lower level of specific enzymes in the differentiated male (testes) and female (ovaries) – gonadal hormone levels differ not only across sexes but also within sexes *across* individuals. Unusually high progesterone and/or estrogen are sometimes associated with low sexual desire in men, but this effect depends on the overall balance between these hormones and the androgens. Because the enzymatic activity within the differentiated gonad tends to favor one set of hormones over the other (androgenic versus estrogenic), it is uncommon to find elevated levels of all gonadal hormones in a given individual. Furthermore, high levels of ovarian (estrogenic) hormones in men are fairly unusual and most often related to a pathophysiological condition.

Two other endocrine abnormalities have been associated with low sexual desire, and both are generally pathophysiologically based. High pituitary prolactin, which may suppress testosterone and modulate hypothalamic function in the brain, is frequently associated with low sexual desire in men. And elevated cortisol, a steroid hormone of the adrenal cortex, has been found to depress sexual desire in men, for example, in men with Cushing's syndrome. Finally, it might be noted that any endocrine abnormality (e.g., thyroid dysfunction) – to the extent that it may disrupt normal HPG function – has the potential to interfere with sexual desire.

General Life Stressors

General life stressors can include any chronic or acute diseases or conditions that interfere with aspects of normal life functioning

General life stressors, whether physiological/physical, psychological, or both, overlap with endocrine-induced pathophysiology, but may also include any chronic or acute diseases or conditions that may interfere with any aspects of normal life functioning. Thus, heart disease, stroke, posttraumatic stress disorder, renal failure, and many other conditions, typically restructure a person's priorities, often placing sexual interest and expression low on the hierarchy. Men with psychobehavioral problems, including depression, anxiety, addiction, eating disorders, and unresolved gender issues – to name a few – are also prone to lowered sexual desire. Whether these conditions act through some common physiological pathway such as elevated cortisol (which itself is associated with stress, lowered testosterone, and diminished desire) is not clear. However, given that sexual expression necessitates an appropriate and priming set of endogenous and exogenous conditions, it is more likely that the lower desire in these men results from a complex interplay of physiological, cognitive, and affective factors. As might be anticipated, removing the stressful condition(s) usually reinstates sexual interest. Yet, procedures designed to treat the "stressing" condition may themselves inhibit sexual desire. Such is the case for some antidepressants, antiepileptics, other neural-modulating medications, radiation and chemotherapies, and surgeries. In some instances, the treatment itself may directly affect the neural and chemical pathways involved in sexual response; in others, a lower health profile and feeling sick and miserable may depress sexual desire.

Relationship and Partner Issues

Relationship and partner issues are sometimes critical to understanding low sexual desire in men, given that factors such as performance evaluation, expectation, and satisfaction naturally come into play with sexual activity. The relationship itself may be the cause of distress, for example, if the relationship is new, undergoing transition (e.g., through the passage of time or due to a newborn), or in jeopardy of dissolution. Specific relationship issues may emanate from anger, frustration, or lack of trust directed toward a partner. Or characteristics of the specific partner may be relevant; for example, a partner may no longer be considered attractive (whether physically or emotionally) or may have developed a sexual dysfunction of her/his own. Or other aspects of the man's sexual response may be relevant; for example, when the man consistently has difficulty keeping an erection, he may experience frustration, which may in turn lead to suppressed sexual interest and subsequent diminished intimacy with the partner (Osborne & Rowland, 2007).

Relationship factors such as performance evaluation, expectation, and satisfaction may contribute to low sexual desire

Such relationship factors are likely to play a significant role in a man's sexual interest, drive, and desired frequency of sexual engagement. As mentioned previously, the man's response *to* his partner and the response *of* his partner introduce potential factors that can explain much of the variance in sexual response, so a clear understanding of the man's low sexual desire may not be possible without some attention to the relationship functioning of the couple. Indeed, this approach assumes a certain reciprocity: Just as sexual interactions affect a variety of other relationship dynamics, so relationship interactions affect sexual dynamics within the couple.

4.1.4   Methods of Treatment

Preparatory Steps: When and Why to Treat and General Treatment Strategies

Low sexual desire is somewhat different from other male sexual problems in that men will not necessarily want or need treatment to alleviate the condition. Specifically, men with low desire may have no interest in changing their situation, particularly if their partner is not perceived as sexually attractive or interested, or if the opportunities for sex are otherwise limited. Furthermore, even when both partners are interested in maintaining an ongoing sexual relationship, the *mismatch* in desired frequency of sex is more likely to lead to treatment than any particular threshold frequency. Specifically, a couple with mutually low desire may be comfortable with monthly intercourse; however, when optimal frequency of sex differs between partners, only then might the issue of low sexual desire arise. This point highlights the relative nature of a diagnosis of low sexual desire: At what point does the patient decide – and the clinician concur – that the desired frequency of sex is too low, about right, or too high?

The mismatch in desired frequency of sex between partners is more likely to lead to treatment than any "threshold" frequency

There are multiple ways to conceptualize low sexual desire and interest

Important to understanding "how to treat" is understanding the etiology of the low sexual desire. In this regard, however, the fields of sexological and psychological health have not fully and consistently differentiated among *types* of low desire. For example, low desire might be conceptualized in several possible ways. It may represent:

- An overall low libido or "spontaneous" (unprompted) interest in sex, that is, the desire is "absent."
- A rearrangement of priorities such that sexual activity is not important at the moment, due to having to deal with more important issues (children, disease, financial problems, etc.). That is, the person's desire is typically present and normal, but has been "depressed" due to specific circumstances.
- Relationship issues, for example, when sexual intimacy becomes entwined with relationship control, such that one person uses a lower desired frequency of sex to control the behaviors of a partner. Eventually, the "controlled" partner may show or express a lack of interest in sex *with this partner* because of the relationship dynamics, even while general interest in sex remains high. That is, desire is "suppressed" with respect to sexual engagement with the particular partner.

As is evident, in the last two categories above, low sexual desire is secondary to other issues, and therefore, these other issues need to be addressed first. Presumably, in most instances, sexual desire may return once the other issues are resolved.

Finally, it is important for the health care provider to differentiate *problems with erection* from *problems related to low desire,* as the patient's everyday language does not make the distinctions afforded by clinical terminology. Thus, a patient might refer to "lack of sex," "not feeling aroused," or "loss of erections," any of which, when probed more deeply, may translate into low sexual desire.

A combination of treatment options is often the best approach for low desire

Several treatment strategies are available for men with low sexual desire, with the choice dependent on the specific nature of the low desire as identified above. These treatments might be summarized as:

- Endocrinological/physiological,
- Psychological counseling dealing with general stressors,
- Psychological counseling focusing on relationship/sexual issues.

As always, such strategies should not be considered in isolation, as a combination of approaches may represent the most effective approach.

Endocrine and Other Biomedical Approaches

Biomedical approaches are appropriate when laboratory tests reveal deficient or abnormal levels of specific hormones. Usually an initial test will analyze at least testosterone – inclusion of prolactin, thyroid function, and fasting lipids and glucose is also a good strategy for assessing possible abnormalities. The blood sample is usually drawn in the morning (when testosterone is high within the circadian rhythm) and repeated at least once before reaching conclusions (see Gooren, 2008; Hackett, 2008, for reviews).

- If such tests indicate no abnormalities, then treatment with androgen has no utility – giving testosterone to an individual having normal testosterone does not increase sexual interest, even in men with low sexual desire.

- If such tests indicate abnormalities in hormones other than testosterone, then these conditions should be treated and brought under control first.
- If such tests indicate morning testosterone levels below 7–8 nmol/L on two separate occasions, then testosterone therapy may be considered. In such cases, the therapy may not only address low sexual desire, but may be important to restoring other functions supported by testosterone, including bone mineral density, cardiovascular function, and emotional health. Testosterone therapy may be continued for these other reasons, even if sexual desire is no longer an issue for the man (e.g., if the relationship ends).

Testosterone therapy can restore many functions driven by hormone deficiency but will not increase sexual interest in men with normal levels

Testosterone Therapy

Assuming testosterone therapy is both indicated and desired, a number of options are available (see Table 4). Three points are key to successful outcomes:

- maintaining fairly constant blood levels of testosterone,
- ease of administration, and
- minimizing adverse effects.

Maintaining constant blood levels is important in testosterone therapy

The first – maintaining constant blood levels – is important for the biological effects of testosterone on sexual desire. The second and third are more important for patient compliance.

Systemically-injected (usually daily intramuscular) formulations tend to produce sizable fluctuations in testosterone levels, and because they are less easy to administer, they seldom represent the first choice. Daily oral preparations require higher doses and are also likely to affect the liver adversely. As a result, transdermal gels and patches – usually applied daily – now represent the preferred method of treatment, although patches may cause skin irritation after repeated application. However, once tolerance and effective doses are established, longer acting subcutaneous pellets lasting for several months typically provide sustained and consistent levels of testosterone.

Table 4
Options for Testosterone Therapy

Route	Formulation	Frequency of administration
Injection	T in oil (various formulations: propionate, cypionate, enanthate, undecanoate)	Every 3 days to once every 10–14 weeks
Oral	T in capsule (various formulations: undecanoate, mesterolone)	1–3 times daily
Buccal	T in tablet-shaped patch applied to upper gum	2 times daily
Transdermal	T in patch or gel form	1–2 times daily
Subcutaneous	T in pellet under the skin	Every 16–26 weeks

Note. Frequency of administration depends on dose and specific formulation, so frequencies indicate the typical range. T = testosterone.

Other Treatments

Pathophysiological conditions other than low testosterone may be responsible for low sexual desire. For example: (1) hyperprolactinemia interferes with sexual desire; (2) various medications may interfere with sexual desire, some through an increase in serum prolactin; and (3) both depression and its treatment through the use of antidepressants may affect sexual desire.

In such instances, treatment of the primary disorder (e.g., tumor-induced hyperprolactinemia) may alleviate the low desire, or selection of another medication with less impact on sexual desire may be considered. Some antidepressants affect sexual desire less than others: For example, mirtazapine, nefazodone, and bupropion are less likely to affect sexual desire.

Method of Action

Androgens have broad effects on men – physiological, physical, and psychological. These hormones, released from the testes and under the regulation of luteinizing hormone secreted by the pituitary gland, bind to receptors located on cells in peripheral body tissue, the brain, and the spinal cord. Through such binding they affect cell activity. Specific to the central nervous system, testosterone binds to neural membranes and in so doing, modulates the activity (potential to respond) of neurons in both sex-specific and nonsexual regions of the brain. Action on the sex-specific brain sites, primarily in the diencephalic/hypothalamic regions, is likely to produce the positive effect on sexual interest and desire. While testosterone exerts a direct effect on sexual desire through this mechanism, it may also affect desire indirectly through its general energizing (and thus positive mood) effects.

Efficacy and Prognosis

Low sexual desire resulting specifically from hypogonadism or low testosterone is highly responsive to testosterone treatment. Furthermore, treatment of hypogonadism with testosterone therapy not only improves sexual desire in the man, but reportedly has positive effects on the couples' overall sexual desire and functioning (Conaglen & Conaglen, 2009).

Transdermal formulations are generally well tolerated, with adverse effects minimized. Positive effects are typically realized within about 1 month of the onset of treatment, although individual variation is substantial. Testosterone levels are typically checked initially every several months, then later at least once a year (often these checks have been accompanied by a prostate-specific antigen [PSA] test for prostate cancer). Treatment predicated on low sexual desire (and not some other effect of low testosterone) may be continued indefinitely or until issues with sexual desire are no longer relevant (e.g., change in relationship status).

Men on testosterone therapy typically show significant improvement in sexual interest and desire; they may also show improvement in their erectile response. Although some of this effect is an indirect one related to improved arousal resulting from improved desire, testosterone also acts directly on penile tissue and therefore may improve erectile capacity as well. Nevertheless, some men whose desire returns to normal after testosterone therapy may still experience erectile problems (e.g., due to cardiovascular disease). These men may be considered for combined testosterone and PDE-5 inhibitor therapy (see Section 4.2).

Counseling Strategies

When low sexual interest appears *not* to be related to a biomedical problem, counseling strategies should be considered. When the low sexual interest/desire is the result of *general stressors*, then a partner's involvement may be optional; in such situations, the man is usually looking for a way to reorder his priorities, perhaps even develop the motivation to seek a new relationship (e.g., after a divorce or death of a partner). If, on the other hand, low sexual desire is tied to *relationship issues*, the partner's involvement will be critical (assuming the man intends to remain in the relationship). In either case, many of the cognitive-behavioral strategies discussed in Section 4.3 (Treatment of Premature Ejaculation) are relevant and can be adapted to augment the approaches mentioned below.

General stress is known to increase levels of adrenal cortisol in the body, and adrenal cortisol and testosterone levels are related: When cortisol is high, testosterone tends to be depressed. Whether or not low sexual desire in men under stress is related to lower testosterone is not clear, but obviously, such men are *not* candidates for testosterone therapy, as their low sexual interest is secondary to other issues. That is, men under significant stress typically restructure their priorities, with sexual interest/desire occupying a lower position on the hierarchy of needs. However, when lack of sexual interest and intimacy begins to negatively affect a couple's relationship (e.g., one partner's sexual interest wanes while the other's is normal), the man (and his partner) may seek general counseling as a step toward reordering life priorities. From the clinician's standpoint, basic cognitive-affective-behavioral techniques used in the counseling for any problem or ongoing crisis are applicable. Such therapies often focus on developing insight into the problem, setting goals for the therapy, establishing motivation to change, realignment of priorities, and implementation of behavioral changes designed to overcome the obstacles to sexual initiative or interaction.

When low sexual interest is the result of relationship dynamics, counseling aimed at *reducing relationship conflict and tension* is appropriate (Maurice, 2007). This tension may be related to issues of relationship control, perceived fairness over accommodation to the other's needs (one partner feels more accommodating/invested than the other), division of labor, perceived prioritization of the relationship by each partner, career paths and priorities, or other problems. All such issues have the potential to affect the emotional response of the partners, to impact sexual dynamics, and to affect sexual desire. For example, in response to one partner's periodic withholding of sex (e.g., due to anger), the other partner may in turn deny or suppress an interest in sex with the partner as a means of countercontrol. In such instances, the basic principles of marital/couples' therapy are applicable. Usually, such therapies include at least some of the following elements:

- setting and agreeing on goals for the therapy;
- developing communication styles and skills;
- understanding of the partner's needs;
- dealing with emotions, including feelings of anger, rejection, guilt, and so on;
- adjusting thought/cognitive processes to support positive changes in behavior;

Counseling strategies are appropriate for men who are experiencing low sexual interest or desire as a result of general stressors

Counseling focused on relationship issues should be used when low sexual interest is related to relationship dynamics

- implementing joint activities for positive relationship building;
- using positive changes in behavior to further support positive cognitions and decrease negative cognitions; and
- dealing with relapse and conflict.

While the above strategies are applicable to general marital/relationship therapy, the infusion of sexual issues may add complexity, as sexual fulfillment lies in the control of the partner and therefore must be negotiated (Osborne & Rowland, 2007). Common scenarios for low sexual interest stemming from the sexual relationship include:

There are several common scenarios for low sexual interest resulting from relationship issues, which complicate strategies used in couples therapy

(1) A mismatch in the desired frequency of sex between partners. In such situations, one partner is often less satisfied with the sexual frequency than the other. The resulting frustration may lead to a variety of response possibilities, from persistence and aggression, to disengagement and suppression or redirection of sex interest/drive by the partner having the greater drive. In such instances, counseling may focus on finding an agreeable compromise, or looking for ways to increase the sexual desire/arousability level of the partner with the lower level of sexual drive.

(2) Relationship conflict leading to emotional distance and/or issues of control. To the extent that the partner with the lower sexual desire uses this "advantage" as a means for controlling the relationship, the partner with the higher sexual desire is likely to feel anger and resentment which may, in turn, lead to withdrawal or to reciprocation by "denying" sexual pleasure to the partner. In such instances, issues of communication, control, and anger need to be addressed in the couple's therapy.

(3) Low level of perceived attractiveness of the partner. As couples age together and life priorities change, attention to one's own physical shape may wane; thus, the characteristics that at one time drew the couple together sexually may no longer exist. At the same time, the emotional bond may not have developed sufficiently to maintain passion in the relationship. In such instances, the couple may take steps to rekindle the relationship through behaviors and situations that increase mutual attraction.

(4) Sexual dysfunction or sexual aversion in the partner. Having a partner who does not enjoy sex is likely to affect the man's own enjoyment of sex, and therefore his interest in sex may decline. In such instances, his sexual desire may be redirected toward another person or object, or it may be suppressed. Therapy is focused on resolving the partner's dysfunction (and any dyadic interactions that may contribute to it) before addressing the man's low sexual desire – such situations of low desire may resolve themselves if/when the partner dysfunction is addressed.

Method of Action

Strategies to address low sexual desire related to relationship issues allow sexual interest to be re-expressed in the relationship

As with couples' therapy in general, the above strategies succeed primarily by altering modes of communication, managing expectations, dealing with emotional tension, rectifying distorted thinking, general relationship building, and channeling behavior into productive outcomes. In essence, these strategies do *not* induce or reinstate sexual desire; rather, they allow sexual interest that has been depressed (due to stress) or suppressed (due to relationship issues) to be re-expressed within the context of the relationship.

Efficacy and Prognosis

Cognitive-affective-behavioral counseling strategies are generally considered efficacious approaches to dealing with an individual's or couple's issues and conflicts (Rowland & Cooper, 2011). While these strategies have the potential to restructure individual and/or relationship functioning, studies that specifically focus on improved or renewed sexual desire as a result of psychosexual or general counseling are rare. Nevertheless, to the extent that such counseling may reverse or counteract depression, anxiety, life stressors, and relationship conflict – factors contributing to low sexual interest – there is real potential for sexual interest and intimacy to reemerge as an important dimension within the relationship. The success of such counseling strategies naturally depends heavily on the motivation and commitment of the individual or couple to address and sort out their issues.

Counseling has the potential to improve sexual interest and intimacy by addressing factors that may contribute to low sexual desire

4.2   Treatment of Erectile Dysfunction

4.2.1   Nomenclature and Definition

For years, problems with erection were known as "impotence"; more recently, to avoid stigmatizing language, the condition has been referred to as "erectile dysfunction" (ED) in the psychosexual literature. This terminology has been widely adopted within the field of sexual medicine with the introduction of oral pharmacological agents such as sildenafil. ED has perhaps gained the widest attention among men's sexual problems and presumably has caused the greatest amount of anguish since the loss of erectile capability has long been associated with a "loss of manhood."

The definition of ED is primarily functional and subjective; it is difficult to identify a quantifiable threshold for classifying this dysfunction

ED is typically defined as the inability to achieve an erection sufficient for penetration or to maintain an erection following intromission. Unlike other sexual problems in men where it is possible to identify a numerical parameter associated with the dysfunction (e.g., ejaculatory latency measured in seconds in men with premature ejaculation, or serum testosterone levels in men with low sexual desire), the definition of ED is primarily functional and subjective: "functional" in the sense that the man is unable to satisfactorily engage in sexual activity (typically with a partner), "subjective" in the sense that the judgment regarding this inadequacy is largely determined according to the patient's own subjective criteria. If the clinician has any doubt regarding the existence of the problem, the patient might be administered one of the sexual assessment forms mentioned in Chapter 1: The SHIM and IIEF, for example, have various cutoff scores that can assist in making a diagnosis (SHIM = 21; IIEF = 25). Since these instruments are based on self-report, they are actually no less subjective than the patient's judgment; however, these instruments use language specific to ED and have demonstrated reliability and validity.

The impact of ED on quality of life often motivates the man and his partner to seek treatment

In addition to the inability to get an erection sufficient for sexual activity and enjoyment, as with other male sexual dysfunctions, ED is typically characterized by distress, concern, anxiety, bother, avoidance of intimacy, or other negative consequences for the patient and/or his partner. Recent studies have clearly documented the negative impact of ED on the quality of life. This impact, of course, motivates the man and his partner to rectify the problem by seeking treatment.

The distinction between biogenic and psychogenic in diagnosis of ED is less important nowadays

Traditionally, a common concern regarding ED is whether its origin is biogenic or psychogenic. In the past, this differential diagnosis was important because strategies for the treatment of psychogenic ED had been developed quite extensively through Masters and Johnson (1970), Kaplan (1979), LoPiccolo (1999), and others, and had been proven effective in helping men regain their sexual response; in contrast, safe, effective strategies for the treatment of biogenic ED were not available. Nowadays, this distinction is less important, as pharmacological solutions are effective for erectile difficulties, no matter the origin. Furthermore, the distinction between psychogenic and biogenic is increasingly blurred, as ED is likely to have both psychogenic and biogenic components. The key to effective treatment lies in understanding how a primarily biogenic problem is likely to impact psychological processes such as confidence and efficacy, or how a primarily psychogenic/anxiety problem is likely to impact physiological function such as autonomic response for erection and ejaculation.

4.2.2   Prevalence

ED is a fairly common problem, affecting as many as 30 million US men and approximately 5–50% of all men depending on their age group (see Lewis et al., 2010). Because erectile response assumes well-functioning vascular and neural systems, the prevalence of ED increases with age, as these systems exhibit age-related diminished responsiveness. Thus, the prevalence may be as low as 10% in men under 40, with incrementally increasing prevalence to over 50% in men over 70 (Lewis et al., 2010).

What is not reflected in these numbers is the percent of ED men whose etiology is primarily psychogenic rather than biogenic – most recent epidemiological studies have not distinguished between psychogenic or biogenic ED. As indicated previously, obtaining such data would be challenging, given the overlap between categories and the often transient nature of psychogenic ED. However, assuming no substantial reason to suppose an increase in psychogenic ED with age, the fact that the prevalence increases from a low of about 10% to as high as 50% in older cohorts suggests that the prevalence of psychogenic ED is no more than 10%, and probably somewhat less,

Prevalence estimates do not distinguish between men whose etiology is primarily psychogenic and those whose etiology is primarily biogenic

4.2.3   Understanding the Mechanisms of Erection

Prior to considering available treatments for ED, a basic familiarity with the physiological process of penile erection is helpful (see Table 5). Penile erection is a vascular process involving increased arterial inflow to the penis, penile engorgement with blood, and decreased venous outflow from the organ;

Table 5
Common Factors Affecting Erectile Response

Proerectile	Antierectile
Penile smooth muscle relaxation	Penile smooth muscle contraction
Increased penile arterial blood flow	Decreased penile blood flow
Occluded penile venal flow	Penile venal leakage
Parasympathetic action	Sympathetic action
Nitric oxide	Adrenalin/epinephrine
Phosphodiesterase-5 inhibitors	Medications such as antidepressants, antihypertensives, etc.

Cardiovascular integrity	Cardiovascular compromise
	    Hypertension
	    Arteriosclerosis
	    Diabetes mellitus

Neural integrity	Neural diseases (e.g., multiple sclerosis, epilepsy)
Relaxation, mindfulness	Anxiety, tension

these processes result in sufficient rigidity for sexual intercourse (Lue, 1992). Whether the penis is erect or flaccid depends upon the physiology of corporal smooth muscle tone, that is, the equilibrium between proerectile and antierectile mechanisms controlling, respectively, relaxant and contractile responses of the smooth muscle cells comprising the penile blood vessels and cavernous tissue. Specifically, the erect penis results from *relaxation* of smooth muscle cells – the vasculature (arteries, arterioles, and capillaries) in the penis opens to allow the increased flow necessary for engorgement. The flaccid penis is characterized by *contraction* of smooth muscle cells – constricted vasculature limits the blood flow to the penis.

Erection results from relaxation of smooth muscle cells under the regulation of the neurological system

The erectile mechanisms operating at the level of the smooth muscle cells in the penis are complex (see Rowland & Burnett, 2000). At the *extracellular level*, neurotransmitters, hormones, and locally released substances from penile tissue both originate and modulate the biochemical signals that produce erection. At the *cell membrane* and the *intracellular level*, second messenger molecules (e.g., cGMP or cAMP) and ions carry out the signal via the action of receptor proteins or enzyme pathways. At the *intercellular level*, the ion channels and gap junctions propagate the signal from one cell to the next. The cumulative input of these factors in response to an erectile stimulus then produces a coordinated physiological response in the penis.

All of these processes are regulated primarily by the neurological system. This system exerts both proerectile and antierectile actions at the central and peripheral levels through adrenergic, cholinergic, and nonadrenergic noncholinergic neurotransmitters. At the central level, several spinal and supraspinal sites have been implicated in the control of penile erection – these operate through various ascending and descending neuronal circuits and involve such neurotransmitters as monoamines, amino acids, neuropeptides, and gaseous molecules. At the peripheral level (autonomic nervous system), the gaseous molecule nitric oxide released primarily from parasympathetic nerve endings coursing to the penis serves as the major proerectile mediator by relaxing smooth muscle cells. In contrast, the sympathetic neurotransmitter norepinephrine released from adrenergic nerve terminals in the penis serves as the major antierectile mediator by contracting smooth muscle cells.

In addition to neurological control, several factors released locally from the corporal tissue of the penis help maintain a tonic flaccid state through vascular constriction (these factors are opposed by vasodilatory substances such as nitric oxide released from vascular endothelium, also known as endothelium-derived relaxation factor or EDRF). Specifically, at the level of the corporal smooth muscle cell, second messenger molecule systems are responsible for stimulating specific biochemical or ionic processes that alter the responsiveness of corporal smooth muscle. Enzymatic pathways (e.g., phosphodiesterase) within the muscle cell may inactivate signal transduction pathways across the cell membrane to suppress erectile function. Intracellular ion homeostasis (i.e., the relative balance between sodium, potassium, chloride, calcium, etc.) may also regulate corporal smooth muscle tone by affecting the membrane potential of the smooth muscle cells.

4.2.4   Risk Factors, Comorbidities, and Other Red Flags

Risk factors may be broadly categorized into one of two domains:
- Pathophysiological, that is, those arising from a general disease state;
- Psychosocial, that is, those arising from a negative affective state, most often related to relationship/partner and/or performance issues.

In addition, endocrine and anatomic anomalies may play a role, but the former tend to affect erectile response indirectly (e.g., through low desire or arousal), and the latter occur only rarely.

Pathophysiological Factors

Given the hemodynamic process of erection, diseases or conditions that compromise cardiovascular function have the potential to interfere with erectile response. Furthermore, since vascular response is under the control of the neural system, neuropathy involving the autonomic nervous system may also interfere with erectile response. Generally, then, as a biogenically based dysfunction, ED is not a specific disease process, but rather just one manifestation of a more general cardiovascular malfunction (Lewis et al., 2008).

> **When ED has a biogenic etiology, it is most often a manifestation of a more general cardiovascular malfunction**

Diseases that affect cardiovascular and/or neural function are typically age-related and sometimes eventually fatal. Thus, the common wisdom in the medical community is that a man having erectile problems due to biogenic reasons usually has far more significant health issues that require treatment. Thus, when a man with cardiovascular problems seeks treatment for ED, it is generally assumed that the compromised cardiovascular response also accounts for the erection problem. However, a man seeking treatment for ED that is deemed biogenic should be further investigated for general vascular or neural disease.

At the level of the vasculature, the problem may be the result of:
- diminished arterial inflow to the penis such that engorgement never fully occurs;
- lack of venous occlusion, resulting in leakage from the venous channels such that the corpora cavernosal bodies of the penis drain the blood pumped in through the arteries, thereby preventing full rigidity;
- a combination of these two processes.

At a more cellular level, *vascular* problems may reflect any one or more diminished capacities, including such processes as loss of elasticity of tissue, decreased responsivity of the smooth muscles that regulate dilation of the vessels, and diminished neurotransmitter production or response resulting in weakened signals to the musculature. The specific disease conditions likely to produce these problems are frequently age-related and include diabetes mellitus, hypercholesteremia, and hypertension, conditions that may result in part from particular long-term lifestyle choices (e.g., smoking, lack of exercise, dietary preferences, and so on). Obesity is also a general risk factor for ED, although it is yet unclear if it represents an independent factor or whether its effect is tied to cardiovascular disease and diabetes. Finally, to the extent that some minority/ethnic groups are at greater risk for these diseases than others, they are also at greater risk for ED. However, actual differences in prevalence of ED appear to be rather small among Hispanic, White, and Black men.

Neurogenic problems typically affect erectile response in a somewhat different manner than vasculogenic problems. With neuropathy, the smooth muscle lining of the vessel walls may be quite capable of responding, but the discrete neural control required to stimulate and control the smooth muscle is disrupted. As with vasculogenic problems, neurogenic dysfunction has many possible origins: degeneration at the synaptic cleft, destruction of specific neural pathways, deterioration of supporting tissue (e.g., myelin glia cells), disruption of neurotransmitter synthesis or metabolism, and so on. Diseases leading to such pathology include Parkinson's, epilepsy, encephalitis, multiple sclerosis, and various other neural degenerative diseases. Strokes, accidents, brain and spinal injury, surgery, and other trauma, depending on their location, extent, and nature, may also affect erectile function either directly or indirectly. Trauma, for example, that directly affects the lower spinal cord is quite likely to disrupt erectile response.

Finally, many *drugs* affect erectile response. And as drugs become more frequently used in treatment, increasing numbers and classes of drugs have been found to impair erection. Thus, one of the first steps in the investigation of ED is determining the use of prescription and over-the-counter medications. Ironically, while many age-related chronic diseases diminish erectile response, the very medications used to manage these diseases may themselves also diminish erectile response.

Psychosocial Factors

Psychological factors related to general life events may indirectly affect erection or may be tied directly to concerns about erection

Psychological factors – the way people think, feel, and behave – affect their erectile response. In many instances, the psychological factors are related to general life events and therefore likely to affect erectile response only *indirectly* – for example, by attenuating sexual desire or arousal. But in other instances, these factors may be tied directly to concerns about getting an erection. When a man has concerns about his "performance," four domains are likely to be affected. These include:

- Cognitive processes: he is likely to focus on negative thoughts related to possible failure, and to focus attention on his own penile response (referred to as "spectatoring"); these cognitive processes typically distract the man from the ongoing sexual stimuli provided by his partner, which in turn interferes with his getting an erection.
- Affective processes: The man is likely to experience anxiety and worry about the consequences of failure; this heightened negative emotional state is strongly associated with an inability to get an erection, perhaps through disruption of the parasympathetic response necessary to mediate erectile response.
- Behavioral strategies: He may make behavioral adjustments to compensate for his fear of failure, including, for example, attempting penetration in a semiflaccid state or ejaculating quickly before losing his erection.
- Relationship processes: The dynamics between the man and his partner may change; for example, the partner feels the focus of interaction becomes getting an erection rather than mutual enjoyment of sex, or either the man or his partner disengages out of frustration or lack of knowing what to do next.

Internal attributions to unsuccessful sexual response can lead to expectation of further failure and set up a vicious cycle

Whether some men possess personality traits or styles that make them more vulnerable to psychogenic ED is not clear, although some differences have been identified. A number of studies (e.g., Fichten et al., 1988; Scepkowski et al., 2004) have shown, for example, that men who are more likely to attribute unsuccessful sexual response to external factors (e.g., not the right moment, not the right partner, not the right situation, etc.) are also more likely to dismiss their "failure" as an anomaly and move beyond it. In contrast, some men internalize their failure, blaming themselves and their own inadequacy. This latter group of men gets trapped in a cycle in which failure, even when occasional, leads to the expectation of further failure, thus setting up a vicious cycle.

4.2.5　Methods of Treatment

What was once the most challenging sexual problem to address through therapy as well as one of the chief causes of distress for men – namely, erectile problems that prevented intercourse – has now become one of the most treatable sexual dysfunctions (see Table 6). This, in part, stems from the introduction of fairly specific and effective oral medications (known generally as PDE-5 inhibitors) that induce smooth muscle relaxation of penile vasculature, allowing engorgement of the corporal cavernosa and subsequent erection (Table 7). At the same time, however, recent clinical and psychophysiological research has been successful in identifying situational, individual, and relationship factors that influence sexual (erectile) response in men. Based on such findings, sex therapists have over the years developed treatment procedures that effectively assist men in overcoming erectile inhibition due to psychological and relationship issues.

> The introduction of oral medications and the identification of situational, individual, and relationship factors that impact erectile response have led ED to become one of the most treatable sexual dysfunctions

Treatments for ED may be briefly summarized as (Table 6):
- Physiological/pharmacological options
  - Use of vacuum devices
  - Oral therapies
  - Intracavernosal injection
  - Penile prosthesis implantation/vascular reconstruction
- Psychosexual counseling
- Combination counseling and physiological/pharmacological strategies

Various treatment strategies have their advantages and limitations, and the choice of one over another will depend, to a large extent, on the goals of treatment and the patient's and partner's preferences. In addition, etiological factors associated with ED may have an impact on the treatment strategy; for example, psychosexual counseling may be included in situations where significant psychogenic factors are implicated, or where relationship issues exist. However, even when psychogenic factors are considered primary, physiological/pharmacological strategies can be used to supplement psychosexual counseling.

Physiological/Pharmacological Strategies
The following biomedical approaches have been listed in order of least to most physiologically invasive. Although vacuum devices are not particularly popular, they are organ specific, time-limited, and have minimal side effects. Oral therapies are more popular and convenient, but affect multiple organs in the body, thereby producing a number of side effects. They are also quite costly and will continue to be so until generic formulations are available.

Table 6
Summary of Treatment Approaches for Erectile Dysfunction and Improved Sexual Satisfaction

Medical	Purported action	Effectiveness	Convenience factor
Physiological/pharmacological			
PDE-5 inhibitors	Induces/maintains relaxation of penile smooth musculature	High	High
Vacuum devices	Increase penile arterial flow through surface vacuum	Moderate	Moderate
Intracavernosal injection	Smooth muscle relaxation in penile vasculatory	High	Low
Penile prosthetics	Implantation of rigid or semirigid core	Moderate	Low
Psychosexual[a]			
Information/ education	Accurate knowledge and realistic expectations	Moderate	High
Improved communication	Convey concerns and desires to partner	High	Moderate to High
Relaxation training	Antagonistic to anxiety and sympathetic dominance	Moderate	Moderate
Sensate focus	Refocus from sexual performance to pleasure	Moderate	Low to Moderate
Cognitive restructuring	Reframe issue, counter myths, reduce negative thoughts	Moderate	Low to Moderate
Affective channeling	Helps channel negative emotions into positive outcomes	Moderate	Low to Moderate
Couples therapy	Improves general relationship functioning	Moderate	Low

Note. PDE-5 = phosphodiesterase-5.
[a]These strategies assume psychological/relationship issues that contribute to or maintain the erectile dysfunction, and their efficacy depends on the extent to which each factor might be involved.

Intracavernosal injection is invasive but has a role for men who do not respond to oral therapies. Surgical prosthesis – both invasive and not easily reversed – is generally considered the final option for the most resistant cases. Vascular reconstruction, a fifth choice, is useful only under very select conditions (Lewis et al., 2008), and it is not discussed in this book.

Table 7
Oral Medications for Erectile Dysfunction

Medication	Trade name	Time to take effect	Duration of effect
Sildenafil	Viagra	30–60 min	About 4 hr
Tadalafil	Cialis	At least 30 min	Up to 36 hr
Vardenafil	Levitra	60 min	About 4 hr

Note. For more information, see PubMed Health (US National Library of Medicine) at http://www.ncbi.nlm.nih.gov/pubmedhealth/

Vacuum Devices

Vacuum devices draw blood into the penis through the use of a manual or battery-powered pump that creates negative pressure on the outside of the penis; the blood is trapped in the penis with the use of compression rings that are placed at the base of the penis, thereby preventing venal outflow. Arterial flow to the penis is increased, and venal outflow decreased, typically resulting in an engorged penis. Vacuum devices have been available for quite some time and have reached a new level of sophistication. They do not require a prescription and may be used repeatedly, helping clients minimize costs after the initial expense. While the process may seem "unnatural" to many couples, and the use of such equipment may seem intrusive to lovemaking, for couples who can comfortably incorporate this process into their coital routine, this method provides a physically *noninvasive* method.

> Vacuum devices increase arterial flow to the penis and decrease venal outflow to produce an engorged penis

Oral Therapies

Oral therapies have become the most popular treatment for men with ED, primarily because of their ease of use and lack of invasiveness compared with other physiological/pharmacological methods. Thus, these new oral pharmacotherapies (sildenafil, tadalafil, vardenafil), typically taken on-demand one to several hours prior to anticipated sex, have not only overshadowed older medical treatments, but changed both the medical and cultural approach to the treatment of ED. Although originally established as a treatment for ED of pathophysiological origin, oral pharmacotherapies offer a range of proven options that can be used to treat sexual problems of varied and even unidentified causes.

> Oral therapies are the most popular treatment for men with ED and can treat sexual problems of varied and unidentified causes

The choice of specific oral therapy may depend on individual need/preference along with the performance characteristics of the specific drug. Sildenafil (Viagra), for example, has proven efficacy for men with ED resulting from a wide range of biogenic causes. Tadalafil (Cialis), on the other hand, has a longer duration than the other compounds and is also available for daily use for those who have intercourse frequently. Vardenafil (Levitra) has received less promotion over the past few years, but has also proven effective through clinical trials. With the 2012 expiration of the patent for sildenafil, less expensive generic options will soon be available.

Mechanism of Action. The current oral therapies approved by regulatory agencies for the treatment of ED are all PDE-5 inhibitors. PDE-5 refers to phosphodiesterase type 5, a specific enzyme responsible for the degradation of cyclic guanosine monophosphate (cGMP) in smooth muscle cells in the lining of the vessels of the corpora cavernosa of the penis. The production of cGMP in the postsynaptic terminal occurs in response to the action of the gaseous neurotransmitter nitric oxide, with the effect of stimulating the dilation of vessels in the penile region. The inhibition of this enzyme by PDE-5 inhibitors such as sildenafil prevents the degradation of cGMP which, in turn, prolongs the stimulatory effect of the cGMP on smooth muscle tissue, thereby increasing blood flow to the penis during sexual stimulation. Thus, the effects of PDE-5 inhibitors on penile tissue are limited to periods of sexual excitation. Various types of the enzyme PDE are found throughout the body, but PDE-5 is fairly limited in its distribution, primarily to the penis and lungs. However, because some PDE-5 inhibitors also affect other types of PDE (e.g., Type 6 in the retina), other tissues in the body may be adversely affected. PDE-5 inhibitors can produce both annoying (e.g., headache, dizziness) and serious (e.g., retinal neuropathy) side effects, and they are contraindicated for people with certain physical conditions or on certain medications, so their use needs to be monitored by a physician.

Oral therapies are successful in 50–90% of men with biogenic ED and also in men with psychogenic ED

Efficacy and Prognosis. Success rates for on-demand or daily use of PDE-5 inhibitors is between 50% and 90% for most men with biogenic ED (Althof et al., 2004). Response rates, however, appear much lower (20–30%) for men with severe diabetes or following radical prostatectomy. In addition, since oral therapies are highly effective for helping men with psychogenic ED regain their erections, these medications can have a role for the treatment of ED in these men as well (see below).

Intracavernosal Injection Therapy

Intracavernosal injection therapy was the most effective treatment predating the introduction of the oral therapies, and it is still used when patients do not respond to PDE-5 inhibitors. A number of preparations (e.g., papaverine, phentolamine, and prostaglandin E_1) are available by prescription, and all

Although effective in eliciting erection, penile injection therapy has several major disadvantages

work through relaxation of smooth muscle tissue lining the vasculature of the penis, allowing engorgement of the penis. These therapies are generally very effective, assuming the existence of smooth muscle responsivity in the corpora cavernosa of the penis (responsivity can be tested by a trial injection in the urologist's office). Despite their effectiveness, the drawbacks are significant: As a needle injection in the penis is required, scar tissue may develop with repeated injections; the risk of priapism (prolonged erection) and its consequences are significant; and pain in the penis may occur.

Surgical Implantation of Penile Prosthetics

Surgical implantation of a prosthetic device is used as a last option when other therapies have not been satisfactory

Surgical implantation of penile prosthetics is a highly invasive procedure generally reserved for men who do not respond to other therapies or are not satisfied with them. For some men with ED (e.g., those suffering severe damage/trauma to the penis), a prosthetic device may be the only option. These devices have varying characteristics: Some are rigid, some semirigid, some use hydraulic inflation, and so on. The devices are designed partly for longevity, typically lasting 10–15 years, and satisfaction among this select group of patients (men with no other recourse) tends to be fairly high.

Psychosexual Counseling

The modern (postanalytic) roots of psychosexual counseling are found in the strategies of Masters and Johnson (1970), Kaplan (1979), LoPiccolo (1999), and others. These strategies, primarily behavioral in nature and based on the newly delineated principles of learning and conditioning current at the time, were aimed at men and women whose sexual dysfunction had its origin in psychological (psychogenic) issues. With early and ungrounded pronouncements that approximately 90% of erectile dysfunction was psychogenic (reliable diagnostic procedures were not available at the time), the use of these techniques became widespread and popular. However, therapists soon realized that these techniques did not work for a sizable percentage of patients, presumably those who in recent times would be identified as patients with biogenic ED.

Today, psychosexual counseling goes beyond the behavioral strategies devised by Masters and Johnson and others from that era, to embrace a more sophisticated approach that attempts to manage not just behaviors, but thought processes (cognitions), emotions, and relationship dynamics. Accordingly, psychosexual counseling continues to play an important role in the treatment of erectile problems. Specifically, psychosexual counseling is appropriate for:

Contemporary psychosexual counseling addresses behavior, thought processes (cognitions), emotions, and relationship dynamics

- Men whose primary problem revolves around anxiety about sexual performance and who prefer a more "natural," drug-free approach.
- Men whose primary problem revolves around anxiety about sexual performance and who are receiving pharmacological therapy. These men will still benefit greatly by strategies that reduce their anxiety and enhance their confidence surrounding sex.
- Men whose primary problem is biogenic and are using a biomedical option but who, with their partner, want to develop a more sexually satisfying relationship.

Preliminary Framework and Considerations

First, the permission, limited information, specific suggestions, and intensive therapy (PLISSIT) model serves as a useful framework when working with ED men and/or their partners. Each step in the PLISSIT model of sex therapy treatment entails a greater level of interaction between the therapist/physician and the couple (Annon, 1974, 1975; Cooper & Rowland, 2005; Rowland et al., 1998). In fact, the first two, or in some cases three, steps can be carried out by a general practitioner or urologist who has taken continuing professional education to become familiar with some basic psychosexual strategies (see Table 8, where this model is applied to men with premature ejaculation).

Second, before beginning psychosexual counseling for ED, the therapist needs to consider whether the partner should be included, whether couples therapy should precede sex therapy, and whether augmentation with available medical treatments should be undertaken. For example, regarding this last point, Althof et al. (2004) recommends medical augmentation when the man with ED has had a lifelong problem, has low self-confidence, significant medical etiology, or a history of unremediated problems despite prior sex therapy.

Therapists should consider whether sex therapy should include the partner, be preceded by couples therapy, and use medical augmentation

Table 8
An Intensity-Gradated Approach to Treatment of Premature Ejaculation

Level of disorder	Suggested cognitive-behavioral interventions	Suggested integration of use of medications
Mild	Education Permission giving to explore non-coital options Specific suggestions for behavioral strategies	Optional
Moderate[a]	Sensate focus exercises/relaxation training Start-stop or squeeze methods Other stimulus reduction methods	Suggested
Severe[a]	Cognitive-affective approaches Relationship issues / couples therapy Relapse prevention Planned follow-up work	Recommended

Note. [a]All of the cognitive and behavioral interventions for the mild level are applicable to the moderate level. Similarly, all the cognitive and behavioral interventions of both the mild and moderate levels are pertinent to the severe level.
Adapted from "Practical Tips for Sexual Counseling and Psychotherapy in Premature Ejaculation," by D. L. Rowland & S. E. Cooper, 2011, *Journal of Sexual Medicine, 8,* pp. 342–352.

Many therapists agree that preliminary treatment with oral medication helps to quickly reestablish a man's self-confidence and reduce his anxiety, clearing the way to deal with other psychological and relationship issues.

Third, as with any type of psychotherapy, psychosexual counseling involves both content and process elements. Content includes the informational, skill- and technique-development, and self-discovery components of the therapy; process involves two elements – first, the strategic use of verbalizations (Busse, Kratochwill, & Elliot; 1999) that define the message process which guides the patient in defining goals and developing self-identified strategies to meet these goals; and second, the manner in which the content elements described above are implemented within the therapist and patient/couple relationship. Many psychotherapists, estimated at close to 40% (Prochaska & Norcross, 2007), use an eclectic or integrative approach, adapted to the patient and his needs (Hackney & Cormier, 2009), an approach that may be especially useful in the treatment of any sexual problems. Process elements of integrative therapy most relevant to ED are:

- developing the therapist–patient relationship;
- expressing empathy, genuineness, and positive regard;
- developing motivation to change, a process that typically involves working through resistance;
- identifying ED-related affects, cognitions, and behaviors (including interactional patterns with partners); and
- supporting self-efficacy.

Fourth, the actual components of current sex therapy strategies for ED have evolved over the past 30 years and include a variety of techniques and methods. All approaches include sex education and dyadic communication as core elements of the therapy. The use of systematic desensitization and anxiety reduction are predicated on the basis that the learning of new and productive behaviors and the elimination of anxiety – a state incompatible with the erectogenic process – will help disinhibit the erectile response. Therapeutic procedures such as sensate focus, relaxation exercises, and other behavioral exercises are typically utilized to facilitate this process. Concomitantly, the highly internalized performance demands of men with ED, as well as the "spectatoring" that often results, may be modified through the use of cognitive restructuring that enables the patient to set expectations that are more realistic and less culturally derived, to develop positive sexual imagery that strengthens self-confidence, and to expand the sexual repertoire to include varied and graduated kinds of stimulation beyond intercourse. Although it is unclear which particular component of these therapeutic processes imparts the greatest benefit, cumulative effects probably accrue, whereby the inclusion of more strategies results in better outcomes. Furthermore, when larger relationship issues emerge as contributing or maintaining factors for ED, augmentation of sex therapy with general couples therapy may become critically important.

Psychosexual Counseling Strategies

In the following sections, a number of commonly used psychosexual strategies are described. Presumably the therapist does *not* approach these as separate components addressed in succession by the patient and his partner, but rather selects and integrates strategies according to need and the goals of the therapy. Since most clinicians are already familiar with the technical details of these strategies, each discussion focuses primarily on the rationale and goal of the strategy.

> Psychosexual strategies should be selected and integrated according to the goals and needs of the therapy

- *Education and information* form the most basic level of intervention, which is intended to correct misperceptions not only about sexual response itself (e.g., the mechanics of erection, the physiological effects of anxiety, and the role of foreplay, including clitoral stimulation, etc.) but also about cultural myths that surround male and female gender roles (e.g., the need for men to take the lead, to always be ready, to last through the night, to be primarily responsible for their partner's satisfaction, and generally to be the "perfect" lover).
- *Communication* between partners is generally considered critical to a satisfying sexual relationship. Assuming that a reasonably effective communication style already exists, the couple may be coached with respect to conveying their wants, needs, and concerns surrounding sexual interaction. This may include expanding the repertoire of activities, discussing what to seek and what to avoid, sharing fantasies, and talking about sex in a nonthreatening (nondemanding) way outside the bedroom.
- *Relaxation exercises* are intended mainly as a form of counterconditioning, on the assumption that the states of anxiety and relaxation cannot coexist. Since anxiety about sexual response interferes with erection, the relaxation induces a state more conducive to getting an erection. Generally, this line of thinking also stems from the well-known inverted U function between anxiety/arousal and performance, such that performance initially increases with increasing levels of arousal; however,

> Relaxation exercises can be used to create a psychophysiological state more conducive to getting an erection

high levels of anxiety/arousal tend to shift attention to the anxiety (and its reduction) rather than to performing/completing the task at hand (consider test taking, giving a presentation, or athletic performance as examples from other areas of performance). As a result, performance begins to drop off as these higher levels are reached; thus the need to replace the anxiety with relaxation.

> Sensate focus encourages the man to focus on experiencing the pleasures of *sensation* instead of focusing on erectile response

- *Sensate focus* reorients the emphasis from the sexual to sensual realm. This technique is often used in combination with relaxation exercises and encourages the man to experience the pleasures of sensation (touch, intimacy) in the absence of the anxiety-inducing attention on sex. To achieve this effect, a ban on sexual activity is often imposed, touching is nongenital focused, and exercises typically last 30–60 min in a comfortable ambience. The exercises progress to include more sexual touching, although the goals of arousal and orgasm are gradual and nondemanding. Overall, the goal is to de-emphasize (the man's concern/obsession about) the penis and replace this with an appreciation of simple intimacy and sexual pleasure.

- *Cognitive restructuring* is often important in helping men who have experienced repeated failures in sexual interactions. Specifically, cognitive schemas are strong differentiators of men with and without sexual dysfunction, including ED (Nobre & Pinto-Gouveia, 2009). Thus, while behavioral approaches focus predominantly on altering the stimulus–response component of ED, cognitive therapies focus on reevaluating and reshaping the interpretation of perceptions and feelings. Moreover, cognitive therapies aim to improve communication between the man with ED and his partner, thereby increasing sexual skills and self-confidence as well as reducing anxiety associated with the sexual activity of the couple as a whole (Barnes & Eardley, 2007). Various cognitive interventions have been empirically supported as effective means for countering distorted thinking and beliefs in general. As such, they can provide a potentially useful approach to countering thought patterns that may contribute to, maintain, or exacerbate ED. Specifically, helpful cognitive strategies that attenuate negativity surrounding ED include (1) identifying faulty or irrational beliefs and attitudes, (2) developing steps to counter them with accurate information, and (3) replacing negative inner dialogue with positive thinking. More detail on these strategies as they apply to the treatment of PE is provided in Section 4.3.4 The general approach as applicable to PE can also be used in the treatment of ED.

> Emotion-focused counseling can help a man identify, express, and work through negative emotions perhaps resulting from sexual dysfunction

- *Affective and emotional responses* are often driven by thought processes, and thought processes reciprocally affect emotional response. Although cognitive strategies often relieve distress, attending to and then directly working through negative emotions may provide an opportunity to resolve emotional issues surrounding the problem. Emotion-focused counseling as a component of overall psychosexual therapy seeks to resolve unpleasant emotions by *conceptionally* treating these emotional states as sources of useful information (Greenberg, 2004) and *operationally* promoting emotional awareness, regulating emotion, and transforming negative emotion into positive emotion (Greenberg, 2004). Accessing and expressing emotion as integrated with cognitive processing is central. Unless these negative emotions are acknowledged, expressed, and worked through one at a time, the therapeutic process may take longer (Teyber, 1997). It is noteworthy that strong emotions can interfere with a patient's ability to make the cognitive and/or behavioral changes essential to therapeutic progress. Research (Ellis, 1992; McMain, Pos, & Iwakabe, 2010) has identified a number of psychotherapy principles that can be used to facilitate emotional awareness, regulation, and transformation, and these may be applied to sexual problems in general, including ED and PE (see Section 4.3 as well).

- *Relationship issues* often emerge as a result of sexual problems, including ones such as ED where one or both partners are sexually dissatisfied or frustrated. Specifically, the inability to satisfactorily complete coital activity negatively affects the relationships men have with their sexual partners (Revicki et al., 2008; Rosen & Althof, 2008; Rowland et al., 1998). The dyadic interactions of the couple, often deeply tied to sexual/ romantic feelings, may be significantly altered as the result of a sexual problem. The intimacy, trust, confidence, and communication between the man and his partner may be compromised due to perceptions of diminished interest, attraction, self-worth, and self-efficacy. In some instances, the relationship issues may warrant a more general couples therapy approach over a specific sex therapy approach. Generally, preceding sex therapy with marital therapy for couples with significant relationship issues leads to better outcomes for the sex therapy, while marital therapy in nondistressed couples does not typically lead to improved sexual functioning. Conversely, sex therapy in nondistressed couples often does lead to improved marital functioning.

Couples with significant relationship issues may require more general "couples" therapy before sex therapy

Although multiple issues as indicated above may be addressed as part of a psychosexual treatment strategy, the number of sessions required may range from one to dozens, depending on the need, severity of the problem, and goals of the therapy. Specifically, in some instances, one or two sessions may be adequate; when the problems are more deep-seated, involving counterproductive cognitive-affective and relationship dynamics, a more intensive regimen may be warranted. Key elements for long term success and satisfaction typically include relapse prevention strategies and periodic follow-up or "booster" sessions.

4.2.6   Combinations of Methods

Therapists want, of course, to use all the available strategies to assist the man and his partner in achieving a sexually satisfying relationship. For this reason, the use of combined psychosexual and pharmacological treatments may prove optimal. For example, men whose ED is primarily biogenic may benefit from guidance regarding relationship and communication strategies that may enhance the effectiveness of the pharmacotherapy. Conversely, men whose ED is primarily psychogenic and who need psychosexual counseling may also realize the benefit of a pharmacological "boost."

Regarding the former group – men whose ED is primarily biogenic – it took little time and even less wisdom to realize that fully functional penises

Men whose ED is primarily biogenic can benefit from attention to psychological and relationship issues that interact with the problem

have limited value and impact in the context of a dysfunctional relationship or one that has been stressed by a major sexual dysfunction. For this reason, it is perhaps not surprising that the adherence rate for oral medications for ED approaches only 50%. The emotional and interpersonal issues that interact with the problem (lack of understanding and communication about sexual issues, blame, distrust, guilt, emotional distance, reduced self-confidence and esteem, and anxiety) have not changed, whether or not a man achieves and sustains erections. However, as the treatment of ED further shifts from the urologist's or sex therapist's office to the office of the primary care physician, attention to relevant psychological and relationship factors may be (benignly) overlooked. This situation is often exacerbated by the typical male focus on genital functioning, leading to resistance to recognize and deal with important emotional and relationship issues. Thus, the burden falls increasingly upon sex therapists and counselors to devise effective, brief, and affordable treatments that can be readily and usefully integrated with the use of the new oral pharmacotherapies. Even before the advent of oral medications for ED, therapies combining medical with psychological treatment, ranging from simple education to more extensive counseling, had been shown to result in greater adherence and overall satisfaction for the couple. Although the number of well-controlled studies indicating improved efficacy using combined therapeutic strategies is limited, clinical impressions suggest that addressing contextual aspects of pharmacological treatment (e.g., relationship concerns) may improve overall treatment satisfaction.

Pharmacological treatment in men with psychogenic ED may improve self-confidence and enable success with psychosexual strategies

Men whose ED is primarily psychogenic can also benefit from a combined pharmacological-psychosexual approach. Men often suffer anxiety after one or several successive sexual performance "failures," although some men appear to be more vulnerable than others in this regard. Such anxiety, accompanied by persistent negative thoughts, can erode the man's sense of self-efficacy and confidence. In using oral therapies in combination with psychosexual counseling, a man can often quickly regain his confidence by knowing that he has the wherewithal to become sexually responsive with his partner. This immediate success enables a reframing of the problem by the therapist and patient, and allows them to develop other strategies such as resistance and resilience.

Psychosexual counseling for ED (presuming psychogenic/relationship issues) tends to produce reasonably high satisfaction rates, typically in the range of 50–70%, that are maintained 12 months or more post treatment. The integration of oral medications into psychosexual counseling for ED is likely to have a further positive impact on satisfaction/success rates. Combined treatment strategies also offer the advantage of decreasing the number of sessions required for successful outcomes, thereby making core elements of sex therapy accessible to greater numbers of couples.

4.3   Treatment of Premature Ejaculation[1]

4.3.1   Nomenclature and Definition

Premature ejaculation (PE) has been known by a variety of names. The classic terminology, *ejaculatio praecox* (literally, precocious ejaculation), was later replaced with *premature ejaculation,* a term that had been entrenched within the clinical community for decades. However, with new cultural awareness and attempts to destigmatize sexual problems, alternative nomenclatures such as *rapid* ejaculation and *early* ejaculation gained ephemeral popularity, as the term *premature* had negative connotations. However, neither of these alternatives successfully conveyed an important aspect of PE, namely that ejaculation occurs prior to some expected or anticipated time. As a result, the terminology *premature ejaculation* has once again become the nomenclature of choice by most researchers and clinicians, although some still prefer to use *rapid ejaculation,* probably the second most common terminology in use.

> The term *premature ejaculation* communicates a key component of the dysfunction: ejaculation occurs prior to an expected or anticipated time

PE is characterized by:

- *A short latency to ejaculation* (usually about 1 min or less) before or following vaginal penetration. About 5–15% of men with PE ejaculate prior to vaginal insertion, a condition referred to as anteportal (literally, "before the entry/gate") ejaculation.
- *The inability to control or delay the ejaculatory response.* This index of "self-efficacy" reliably differentiates men with PE from those without PE (Rowland, Patrick, Rothman, & Gagnon, 2007); specifically, men with PE typically report little to no ability to control the timing of their ejaculation, in contrast to men without PE who typically report a higher level of control on the same scale.
- *Distress, bother, or some other negative consequence such as avoidance of intimacy.* All consensus definitions of PE have included some type of negative influence on the man's life, whether described as distress, bother, upset, frustration, interpersonal difficulty, relationship difficulty, decreased enjoyment of lovemaking, and so on. Recent studies have shown that most men with PE report their lives or relationships have been negatively affected by this condition, at a level comparable to that of men with ED. Men with PE report their partners are adversely affected as well, and their partners generally verify this (Rowland et al., 2007; Symonds et al., 2003). Such consequences typically drive men and their partners to seek treatment.

> All contemporary definitions of PE include reference to the negative impact it has on the man's life

4.3.2   Prevalence

Somewhere between 15% and 30% of men report having PE at some point in their lives, with the range in rate dependent in part on the specific criteria used for classification, including the degree to which the man is distressed by the condition. Specifically, higher rates may include men who, while reporting

---

[1] This section 4.3 was coauthored by Stewart Cooper.

short ejaculatory latencies, are not particularly bothered by it and therefore less likely to seek help.

Although data are limited, estimates are that about 75% of men with PE have primary (or lifelong) PE (McMahon, 2002), and that the other quarter have acquired it at some point during their sexual lives. Acquired PE may result from either pathophysiological or psychological factors. About a third of men with PE also report having erection problems, so it is essential to determine which problem is primary and which is secondary (the ED or the PE), as treatment needs to begin with the primary problem. The relationship may, of course, be bidirectional in some instances.

4.3.3   Risk Factors, Comorbidities, and Other Red Flags

Physiological Factors
For most men with PE, no obvious pathophysiology exists; that is, no underlying problem in structural or functional anatomy, physiology, or biochemistry can be identified. When PE does have a pathophysiological origin, it is usually fairly easy to identify and is likely to surface during a medical history and exam. For example, among the conditions commonly associated with PE are problems in the lower urinary tract (such as prostatitis and urethritis) and endocrine problems, particularly hyperthyroidism. Sometimes, however, the site of the pathophysiology may be far removed from the pelvic or genital area: For example, cerebrovascular accidents have sometimes been linked to PE. Specific drugs may sometimes induce PE, though not necessarily with any reliability. For example, use of L-DOPA, pimozide (an antipsychotic used to control tics), amphetamine, heroin, and over-the-counter drugs that mimic sympathetic activation have on occasion been associated with PE.

Inherent differences in response tendencies may predispose men to respond with shorter or longer ejaculatory latencies

Most current thinking views ejaculatory latency as showing "natural" variation across individuals, suggesting some degree of "hardwiring" of the ejaculatory reflex and latency. It is quite plausible to assume that, as with most biobehavioral responses (e.g., eating, emotion), inherent differences in response tendencies exist and that, for the specific biobehavioral response of ejaculation, men do possess predispositions to respond with shorter or longer latencies (see Figure 2). However, the actual inherent physiological properties that differentiate men with PE from men with more typical latencies are unknown. Men with PE, for example, sometimes complain of penile hypersensitivity, and several studies have demonstrated greater sensitivity in such men. But other studies have shown that men with *low* penile sensitivity may show short latencies as well. If PE is not due to the hypersensitivity of the sensory system, then perhaps the response system in PE men is more easily triggered due to greater responsivity of the reflex or a lower ejaculatory threshold. While several studies support this idea, no consensus currently exists about the role of these factors in PE. Even so, as with most biobehavioral responses, inherent (biological) tendencies probably do not *determine* the latency of ejaculation but rather *set the range* for responding, with more proximal factors such as context, partner, level of arousal, and so on influencing when within that range the response actually occurs (Paick, Jeong, & Park, 1998; Rowland, 1998).

Psychological Factors

Surprisingly little is known about *psychological* factors related to PE. The question whether men with PE are somehow fundamentally different from other men has long been a topic of interest. For example, early research suggested that men with PE were narcissistic and uncaring toward their partner (as discussed in Masters & Johnson, 1970), an idea that has received little or no support from contemporary analysis (Rowland et al., 2004). Yet, several studies do suggest that men with PE may have heightened social-cognitive or affective vulnerability.

Specifically, anxiety, a construct considered central to many psychological disorders, has also been postulated to have a role in psychogenic sexual dysfunction, including premature ejaculation. For example, men with PE on average display more trait-based anxiety and depression (Corona et al., 2004; Munjak, Kanno, & Oziel, 1978) than the general population, and men with PE approach psychosexual stimuli (such as visual sexual stimulation) with greater overall negative affect than controls (Rowland, Tai, & Slob, 2003). Furthermore, these negative emotions (such as embarrassment, guilt, and anxiety) appear to be fairly deeply entrenched in the individual. What remains unresolved is the reason or cause for the anxiety itself – is it genetically or developmentally predispositional (e.g., Cooper, Cernovsky, & Colussi, 1993)? Is it general anxiety tied specifically to social interaction? Is it the consequence of feelings of inadequacy and failure with the sexual partner? Is it the fear of future poor sexual performance?

> On average, men with PE exhibit more trait-based anxiety and depression, displaying greater negative affect in response to psychosexual stimuli

Perhaps not surprising in view of the emotional characteristics and disturbances discussed above, recent research has identified men with PE as having a higher level of alexithymia (Michetti et al., 2007). Alexithymia is a disorder characterized by an inability to recognize, interpret, and verbalize signs of emotional arousal in oneself or others – that is, such persons are "not as in touch with themselves emotionally." Men with PE were particularly high on one specific subscale: namely, a "stimulus bound externally oriented cognitive style." Such men, rather than relying on their own inner feelings, depend more heavily on external cues for expression and action (Taylor, Bagby, & Parker, 1999). Not inconsistent with the above findings, several studies have shown a link between PE and social anxiety/phobia (Corretti, Pierucci, De Scisciolo, & Nisita, 2006; Figueira, Possidente, Marques, & Hayes, 2001).

One interpretation for the above associations is that heightened risk for affective problems, inhibited social confidence, and amplified impact of external influencers – including social norms and/or partner feedback – constitutes specific vulnerability in the realm of "social-affective" functioning, at least for a subpopulation of men with PE. Although the social-affective functioning of men with PE tends not to fall in the clinical range, this social-affective vulnerability may heighten the probability for developing and intensifying negative (and counterproductive) thought patterns – patterns known to contribute to, maintain, or exacerbate functional impairments in many psychological realms, including PE (Patrick, Rowland, & Rothman, 2007).

The Relationship Dimension

More so than the other male sexual dysfunctions, PE is considered a couple's problem: The dysfunction does not typically exist outside the man's relationship. For this reason, treatment of the couple is often strongly advocated for men with PE, particularly when a committed partner is involved. Furthermore, the propensity toward rapid ejaculation may be increased by a partner who has a sexual aversion, exhibits sexual avoidance, or is concerned about sexual pain. Although such partner issues may lead men to ejaculate rapidly, the PE in this case is actually secondary to the partner's dysfunction. Treatment would therefore focus on the partner's problem and the overall relationship rather than just the man's ejaculatory response.

> **PE is generally considered a couple's problem and therefore treatment that includes the partner is recommended**

More often than not, partners of men with PE share in the distress of the patient and experience sexual dissatisfaction as a result of the man's problem. For this reason, female partners of men with PE are often motivated to encourage their men to seek treatment (Moreira, 2005).

4.3.4   Methods of Treatment

A number of treatment options are available for men with PE (Table 9). These may be summarized as:
- Psychosexual
  - Behavioral
  - Cognitive-affective
  - Relationship
- Pharmacological
  - Topical ointments and creams
  - Oral-based neurotransmitter reuptake inhibitors
  - Combined pharmacological approaches
- Combined psychosexual and pharmacological

Surgical transection of the penile sensory (dorsal) nerve has been reported in several countries for men with PE who are unresponsive to other forms of treatment. However, such procedures are not widely accepted, practiced, or advocated in most medical circles.

Psychosexual Approaches: General Framework and Historical Perspective
Psychosexual approaches to PE may be conceptualized as behavioral, cognitive-affective, and relationship-based. In reality, the therapist or clinician integrates all three aspects into an overall therapeutic strategy that addresses issues as they emerge and suggests possible strategies and tasks to help resolve them. Furthermore, these elements are embedded within the larger clinical/therapeutic context, which deals with a variety of other interpersonal and therapist–client issues.

> **Mental health clinicians can provide psychosexual treatment; a specialist is often not required**

Clinical experience indicates that many men with PE can benefit from a brief course of psychosexual counseling (e.g., two to eight sessions, each typically 50-min long), targeted at functional improvement and, if appropriate, relationship coping. Additional effectiveness and efficacy can sometimes be obtained from the flexible use of the timing of the sessions (e.g., varying their spread, with weekly meetings at first, but less frequent meetings as progress is made) as well as length of sessions (e.g., longer 90–120 min sessions at the beginning when working with the patient and his partner, and 30 min sessions later on, when the focus is to adjust the use of techniques and

Table 9
Therapeutic Strategies for the Treatment of Premature Ejaculation

Method	Description	Purported action	Advantages	Disadvantages
Psychosexual				
Behavioral	Stop-squeeze/pause	Reduce penile stimulation	Learn control over response	Requires partner
Cognitive-affective	Reframe problem Attend to sensations	Accurate expectations and strategies to match	No adverse effects	Unknown efficacy
Relationship	Couples therapy	Improved communication, sexual repertoire, etc.	Improved sexual and relationship satisfaction	Requires partner Cost factor high
Pharmacological				
Oral therapies	Reuptake inhibitors	Affects central serotonin	Proven efficacy	Symptomatic cure Adverse effects
Topical ointments	Applied to penis	Reduce sensory stimulation	Localized effect	May affect partner genital sensitivity
Combined drug	Reuptake inhibitors PDE-5 inhibitors	Affects central serotonin Increased penile blood flow	Proven record for men with ED + PE	Adverse effects
Combined methods				
	Drug plus counseling	Multiple effects	Holistic approach	High cost factor Not well documented

Note. ED = erectile dysfunction; PDE-5 = phosphodiesterase-5; PE = premature ejaculation.

to incorporate additional interventions). Except for highly treatment-resistant cases, psychosexual treatment does not require a specialist in the field, as few psychotherapists focus exclusively on treating patients with sexual dysfunctions, and those that do may not be locally available. Mental health clinicians who have obtained education and supervised experience in treating men with PE would constitute the typical referral resource when the clinician is unable to make progress.

For men with PE, the initial contact with a psychotherapist may begin with an assessment session, after which the patient then decides whether to pursue counseling. This two-step process may reduce the barriers for many of them to seek psychological treatment, as the commitment needed to participate in a single session is less than an upfront commitment to a full course of treatment.

As with any type of psychotherapy (noted earlier in Section 4.2), psychosexual counseling involves both content and process elements. Content includes the informational, skill- and technique-development, and self-discovery components of the therapy; process involves two elements:

(1) The strategic use of verbalizations, which guide the patient in defining goals and developing self-identified strategies to meet these goals (Busse et al., 1999).

(2) The manner in which the content elements mentioned above is implemented within the therapist and patient/couple relationship (Hackney & Cormier, 2009).

Process elements of integrative therapy most relevant to psychosexual counseling for PE are (1) developing the therapist–patient relationship; (2) expressing empathy, genuineness, and positive regard; (3) developing motivation to change, a process that typically involves working through resistance; (4) identifying PE-related affect, cognitions, and behaviors (including interactional patterns with partners); and (5) supporting self-efficacy. Critical elements of these are treated briefly later in this chapter.

Outcomes can be optimized by involving the partner in the treatment process

An important motivating factor for the "PE couple" to seek treatment is the negative impact and reduced sexual satisfaction for both the man and his partner. Accordingly, it is important that PE is typically regarded by clinicians as a *couple's* problem and that, whenever possible, the partner is included in the treatment process to help optimize outcomes (Althof et al., 2010; Rosen & Althof, 2008). Partners who are not involved in the management of PE may resist the ensuing change in sexual dynamics, thereby countering the potential positive effects of treatment. Conversely, a cooperative and supportive partner can enhance the man's self-confidence and esteem, and assist in developing more ejaculatory control. This, in turn, can contribute to an overall improvement in the couple's sexual relationship and reduce the negative impact on their quality of life.

Involving the partner may not be possible in some situations – for example, a newly forming relationship, engagement with casual sexual partners, etc. However, treatment for PE in such cases can still be successful. Furthermore, partners in even relatively short-term relationships are often willing to participate in a session or two if requested, as they would function in a collateral supportive position, rather than as the focus of treatment (Perelman, 2003b).

Masters and Johnson's behavioral approach has been considered a mainstay treatment for the past 40 years

For many decades, PE had been considered an intrapsychic disturbance, and intrapsychic explanations have traditionally (though not exclusively) suggested the need for a psychoanalytic treatment approach. To the extent that psychoanalytic approaches delved into the developmental sexual histories of the patient, they may have been successful in providing some patients with insight into their problem (Rowland & Cooper, 2011). Psychoanalytic interpretations had often focused on underlying dynamics, with repressed hostility toward women and fears of overwhelming loss of the self in the sexual experience as the most commonly assumed causes. Gestalt perspectives highlighted barriers to awareness of one's own sexuality, and transactional theories focused on power issues surrounding the couple's interactions. However, the wide variation in potential intrapsychic explanations, together with a lack of standard treatment protocols, rendered psychoanalytic strategies nonreplicable and questionable in terms of treatment success. Against this backdrop, Masters and Johnson (1970) reframed PE as a learning/behavioral problem, where the dysfunctional response – presumably developed through conditioning – could be modified through appropriate counterconditioning measures of stimulus control and reinforcement. For the past 40 years, their behavioral approach – which included interactive elements with the partner – was considered the mainstay treatment for this dysfunction. Their approach, as well as that of Kaplan (1974), most frequently used behavioral strategies designed to attenuate or counter penile stimulation, respectively the "stop-squeeze" technique described by Masters and Johnson and the "start-stop" method described by Kaplan. These techniques involved engaging in sexual foreplay just prior to the point of ejaculation and then either squeezing the head of the penis or stopping sexual activity until the urge to ejaculate subsided (see Rowland et al., 1998).

Psychosexual Approaches: Behavioral

To be considered empirically supported, a therapeutic approach must be backed by:

- at least two studies showing it to be more effective than a waiting-list control group; or
- at least two studies demonstrating effectiveness but which may have flawed sample heterogeneity; or,
- a series of case studies in which the patient sample was clearly specified and the treatment procedure described in a detailed manual.

Two behavioral approaches to the treatment of PE, the stop-squeeze method and the start-stop method, come close to meeting these criteria (Hawton, 1989; Hawton, 1992).

The stop-squeeze method was first developed by Semans in 1956 and later adopted by Masters and Johnson (1970) in their sex therapy clinic. This method calls for the man to signal his partner when he feels his ejaculatory urge building. The couple then stops the sexual stimulation and the partner applies manual pressure to the glans of the penis until the urge is reduced, though not to the point where the erection is lost. Different amounts of time for the squeeze have been advocated, but there is no current evidence to support any particular duration. Rather, an individualistic approach which balances urge reduction while maintaining a moderate level of sexual arousal appears most effective (Zilbergeld, 1993). With this strategy, the man pays careful attention to his sexual sensations and stops activity well before ejaculatory inevitability. The stop-squeeze method is typically employed first with masturbation, in a cycle that includes three pauses before orgasm. Once successful, the method then progresses to a cycle of two pauses with intercourse in the female superior position, and finally to a cycle of two pauses with intercourse in the lateral position. This training requires an almost exclusive focus on the man's experience of sexual stimulation and needs.

Kaplan (1974) subsequently developed the start-stop behavioral approach to the treatment of PE men. The fundamental difference between the start-

The stop-squeeze and
start-stop methods
are moderately
successful in
providing men with
PE techniques that
enable control over
ejaculation

These behavioral
procedures also
promote interactive
efforts between the
couple

stop and stop-squeeze methods is that the former utilizes a pause rather than a squeeze at the onset of ejaculatory inevitability. Kaplan preferred this approach because it better simulated the final behaviors required to prolong ejaculation latency during intercourse. These approaches – although not delivering completely on their promise – were moderately successful in attuning men to premonitory ejaculatory response and developing techniques that enabled many to gain control over the timing of their ejaculatory response. Equally important, they framed the problem as one that might be solved best through the interactive efforts of the couple.

In addition to the classic approaches above, several other behavioral strategies have been suggested. For example, the couple could be encouraged to experiment with the partner (e.g., female) superior or lateral positions as these typically provide men with a greater sense of ejaculatory control. Couples could also be advised to engage in mutual masturbation and then oral sex prior to coitus (depending on the acceptability of the sexual behaviors to the couple). Other suggestions include slowing down during intercourse, breathing deeply, having shallower penile penetration, or moving the pelvis in a circular motion. A related strategy with some preliminary research support involves strengthening the pelvic floor muscles through 20 sessions of Kegel exercises; pelvic muscles are presumably involved in the control of the ejaculatory reflex, and such exercises have been used with some success in the control of urinary and fecal incontinence (La Pera & Nicastro, 1996).

Finally, sexual behaviors associated with PE may sometimes (though not always) work against increasing ejaculatory latency, and therefore the behavioral treatment strategies may counteract these PE-supporting behaviors. However, treatment strategies are also intended to introduce new, alternative behaviors designed to optimize ejaculatory latency and control.

Method of Action

Behavioral techniques focus primarily on reducing the intensity of penile stimulation and/or reducing the response to the stimulation. To the extent that the ejaculation represents a stimulus-response (S-R) reflex, these approaches make inherent sense. Even today, however, an underlying psychophysiological explanation for the inhibiting effects of the "squeeze" technique on ejaculation has not been elucidated. Furthermore, behavioral approaches attempt to replace counterproductive behaviors – for example, attempting to reduce arousal through distracting thoughts – with more effective strategies such as attending more closely to the premonitory sensations leading to ejaculation or providing greater partner stimulation by varying precoital sexual activities.

Clinicians using
behavioral
techniques
conceptualize
ejaculation as a
stimulus-response
reflex

Efficacy

Masters and Johnson's (1970) initial report of only a 2% short-term failure rate and 3% long-term failure revolutionized a field that had been floundering with poor results in the treatment of PE. Subsequent studies, however, have reported much lower success rates, typically in the neighborhood of 50–60% (Grenier & Byers, 1995; Hawton, 1989; Madakasira & St. Lawrence, 1997; Metz, Pryor, Nescavil, Abuzzahab, & Koznar, 1997). Undoubtedly, the success rates reported by Masters and Johnson were influenced by selection bias. Kaplan also reported high success rates, as high as 80–90% in men with pri-

Behavioral
techniques are
neither harmful nor
painful, and have
no negative side
effects, but they do
require the partner's
cooperation

mary, generalized PE (i.e., with all partners and often during masturbation). Although subsequent studies were less successful than Masters and Johnson's or Kaplan's initial reports (Spector & Carey, 1990; Waldinger, Rietschel, Nothen, Hengeveld, & Olivier, 1997), behavioral approaches to the treatment of PE have, on the whole, generally shown moderate efficacy in terms of both ejaculatory control and improved sexual satisfaction (Rowland & Slob, 1992). Although behavioral approaches to PE have been criticized as lacking long-term efficacy, long-term success rates for PE treatment have simply not been adequately investigated, and the reasons for purported failures (about 50% long term) remain largely unknown. For example, it is not known whether relapse occurs because behavioral techniques become less effective with continued use, or because couples merely cease using them once the novelty has worn off. On the other hand, behavioral techniques offer certain clear advantages: They are specific to the problem, are neither harmful nor painful, and impart no negative side effects. Once learned and incorporated into lovemaking, these techniques can help men gain control of their ejaculatory response. On the negative side, behavioral techniques typically require significant cooperation of the partner; entail greater effort, expense, and time on the part of the patient; and tend to have less well documented efficacy (Rowland et al., 1998).

Parameters Affecting Treatment Outcomes

The general procedures described above rather than any of their specific variations have received the strongest empirical support. Much of the research on the stop-start and stop-squeeze methods has attempted to identify parameters that maximize their treatment efficacy. These include:

(1) *The frequency and intensity of treatment.* Most therapists no longer endorse the long-term treatments prescribed by early behavioral approaches, but rather limit treatment to one or several sessions, with periodic follow-up to ensure compliance and handle relapses.

(2) *Treatment formats.* A number of alternative formats for the treatment of PE have been investigated, including the use of bibliotherapy, group versus individual therapy, and couples versus individual therapy. Clinical research supports the use of bibliotherapy combined with some type of therapist contact for men having high motivation and relatively straightforward PE without comorbid disorders (Hawton, 1989). However, men with PE who have complicating factors such as individual or relationship difficulties or concomitant erectile problems benefit less from reliance on this format. Data on group (versus individual) treatment for PE are mixed. Some investigations have found the two formats equivalent, whereas others have not (Madakasira & St. Lawrence, 1997; Marks, 1981). Use of group therapy is primarily a matter of the couple's preference and openness to receiving treatment in a group setting.

(3) *Inclusion of the partner.* Behavioral treatment of PE in an individual format is generally not as successful as working with couples. Individual treatment in the absence of a partner precludes the opportunity to practice behavioral strategies in situ. Still, instances arise when individuals are bothered by their PE and thus seek treatment without

a partner. In such instances the stop-squeeze and start-stop techniques may be adapted to masturbation, especially when intensity of arousal is enhanced by adding a lubricant and using erotic literature or fantasy (Hawton, 1985). This self-sexuality training can be complemented with education about the female and male sexual response cycles. Training of ejaculatory control through masturbation typically entails a goal of 15 min of sexual stimulation of varying intensity before reaching orgasm.

Psychosexual Approaches: Cognitive-Affective

Currently, there are no empirically supported studies showing efficacy for cognitive-affective approaches *specific to the treatment of PE*. However, psychosexual therapy has the potential to reduce or attenuate specific maladaptive cognitive-affective-behavioral patterns that may complicate a dysfunctional sexual response.

Cognitive therapies improve couples' communication, help develop sexual skills and self-confidence, and reduce anxiety

While behavioral approaches focus predominantly on altering the stimulus–response component of PE, cognitive therapies focus on reevaluating and reshaping the interpretation of perceptions and feelings. Moreover, cognitive therapies aim to improve communication between the man with PE and his partner, thereby increasing sexual skills and self-confidence as well as reducing anxiety associated with sexual activity of the couple as a whole (Fichten et al., 1988). Specifically, helpful cognitive strategies that attenuate negativity surrounding PE include (1) identifying faulty or irrational beliefs and attitudes, (2) developing steps to counter them with accurate information, and (3) replacing negative inner dialogue with positive thinking.

One cognitive approach having particular relevance to the treatment of PE is that of "mindfulness" (sometimes referred to as mindfulness-based cognitive therapy [MCT]), the idea of bringing one's complete attention to the ongoing moment-to-moment experience. Mindfulness exercises help the individual decrease irrelevant, distracting, or negative thoughts such that the individual can become fully engaged with the sensations, feelings, and experiences of the moment. For the man with PE who may have unwittingly used distraction as a means of attempting ejaculatory control, the mindfulness approach takes an opposing tack, focusing cognitive energy on a relaxed, sometimes removed, meditation-like state attentive (in a nonemotional way) to the sexual/sensual feelings of the moment. Such an approach can enable a man with PE to become more cognizant of cues related to arousal and impending ejaculation.

Dealing With Faulty Beliefs

A man with PE may have faulty beliefs that do not necessarily reflect the needs and desires of his partner

A man with PE may hold a number of faulty beliefs, such as thinking that in order to pleasure himself and his partner sufficiently he must engage in full sexual intercourse that lasts a long time and involves continuous thrusting. These beliefs, however, may not reflect the needs and desires of his partner. In addition, before seeking treatment, some men with PE may have adopted coping strategies that can, paradoxically, worsen the condition and/or become part of the problem – for example, by focusing on nonsexual, distracting stimuli (Rosen & Althof, 2008). Therefore, one key goal of cognitive therapy is for the patient to learn to refute faulty beliefs and replace them with more accurate and beneficial ones.

Dealing With Distorted Thinking

Distorted thoughts typically reinforce negative thinking or emotions and may make the patient feel worse. Furthermore, each time a distorted thought is allowed, it strengthens and reinforces the corresponding dysfunctional belief. For example, a man who has experienced rapid, uncontrolled ejaculation on several occasions may begin to develop high anxiety about any and all sexual interactions with his partner; he may assume that the pattern will repeat itself and obsess about "what if it happens again." Helping the couple establish behaviors and thoughts that counter such dysfunctional patterns is a critical and powerful aspect of cognitive therapy. A variety of cognitive interventions to counter distorted thinking are available, four of which are briefly described below: Desibels intervention, counters therapy, rational-emotive behavioral therapy (REBT), and self-instructional techniques. These interventions have been empirically supported as effective means for countering distorted thinking and beliefs in general and may be used to counter beliefs that may contribute to, maintain, or exacerbate PE.

Using Prescripted Strategies. The *Desibels* stands for DESensitizing Irrational BELiefs and is based, in part, on research indicating that patients' awareness and mindfulness of their disturbances in thinking will lower their feelings of distress. Moreover, patients can use a multiple-step process involving 10 min each day, to identify and change beliefs that maintain or exacerbate their problem, in this case the PE.

> **"Counters" therapy asks the patient to identify counterarguments to his PE-related irrational belief**

Similar to Desibels, Counters involves the patient's identifying, both orally and in writing, counterarguments to each PE-related irrational or problematic belief. McMullin and Giles (1998) provide six parameters to assist patients in developing counters specific to meeting their therapeutic goals. Counters must directly contradict the false belief, be believable statements of reality, be concise, be created and owned by the patient, and be stated (either externally or heard mentally) with assertion and emotional intensity. Finally, developing more counters leads to greater effectiveness. Patients can practice these counters both in the therapy sessions and at home as a means of affirming the value of the counter.

Rational-Emotive Behavior Therapy. Rational-emotive behavior therapy (REBT), developed in 1955 by Albert Ellis, focuses on people's tendencies to create their own emotional difficulties and takes into consideration the interactions of human thoughts, feelings, and actions (Hackney & Cormier, 2009). REBT is based on the principle that a person's past experiences shape his or her belief system and thinking patterns. Patients with PE may, for example, form illogical, irrational thinking patterns that become the cause of both their negative emotions and further irrational ideas. REBT helps patients uncover these irrational beliefs and replace them with rational beliefs and thoughts, in order to relieve emotional distress. REBT is based on the understanding that the responsibility for people's feelings of upset, anxiety, and/or depression lies not with the events taking place but rather with client's irrational beliefs. The initial phase of REBT enables the patient to recognize, record, analyze, and modify these irrational cognitions. The second phase is aimed at identifying and modifying the dysfunctional attitudes that give rise to irra-

> **The irrational beliefs of men with PE are often embedded in culture**

tional cognitions. The goal of REBT is, therefore, achieved by disputing the patient's irrational beliefs and converting these irrational beliefs into rational ones. With respect to men with PE, irrational (and often self- or performance-destructive) thoughts are often embedded in culture. For example, in the United States, these thoughts may include "I must be the perfect lover" or "I must be a successful lover or I am a failure." Men in other cultures, such as Japan, may hold self-destructive beliefs such as "I should always control my feelings."

Self-Instructional Training. Similar to REBT, self-instructional training encourages people to replace negative thoughts and self-defeating inner dialogue with positive thoughts. With respect to ejaculation, centrally mediated processes, including those that control the level of psychological sexual arousal, affect the ejaculatory threshold. Accordingly, conscious cognitive (e.g., attention focus), behavioral (e.g., position and timing adjustments) and affective (e.g., emotional excitement) treatment strategies may modulate arousal sufficiently to influence (i.e., increase, in the case of PE) the ejaculatory threshold and latency (Rowland, 2010; Rowland & Crawford, 2011). Helpful cognitive strategies that attenuate negativity surrounding PE include identifying faulty or irrational beliefs and attitudes, developing steps to counter them with accurate information, and replacing negative inner dialogue with positive thinking. In addition, use of symbolic and covert modeling tools may assist patients in developing and implementing effective self-instruction.

Affective Issues

Affective domain interventions, as illustrated by emotion-focused therapy (EFT), seek to promote emotional awareness, regulate emotion, and transform negative emotion into positive emotion (McMullin & Giles, 1998). Accessing and expressing emotion as integrated with cognitive processing is central. Specifically, while cognitive strategies often relieve distress, strategies focused on emotion – for instance, attending to and then directly working through negative emotions, particularly those that lead to counterproductive behaviors such as avoidance – may provide a needed opportunity to resolve emotional issues surrounding the problem.

Sadness-anger-hurt and anger-sadness-shame are two emotional sequences common among men with PE

EFT, a short-term psychosexual counseling approach to working with men and couples with PE, aims to resolve unpleasant emotions by considering these emotional states as sources of useful information. Recent research (Bandura, 1977; McMullin & Giles, 1998) has identified a number of general psychosexual counseling principles that can be used to facilitate emotional awareness, regulation, and transformation.

Among patients with PE, two 3-phase emotional experiences are common: sadness-anger-hurt and anger-sadness-shame. Both patterns can be seen as a triad of emotional rules to protect against hurt, with one predominant emotion usually driving the person's coping mechanism. Although the other emotions are equally important, they are often avoided and/or perceived as unallowable or acceptable. For example, in sadness-anger-hurt, the predominant feeling is sadness, but this feeling is often connected to "denied" anger. Unless these related emotions are acknowledged, expressed, and worked through one at a time, progress may take longer. It is noteworthy that strong emotions can interfere with a patient's ability to make the cognitive and/or behavioral changes essential to therapeutic progress.

Method of Action and Efficacy

Substituting counterproductive behaviors and beliefs that may complicate the dysfunctional response with positive therapeutic strategies is an important part of treatment. It is equally important to develop deliberate strategies to channel emotions into productive outcomes, to challenge negative coping strategies, and to prevent and/or deal with relapses to improve general sexual and relationship satisfaction. Although the cognitive-affective strategies are not likely to have a direct impact on the latency to ejaculation in men with PE, when used in combination with the behavioral techniques described previously, they may enhance the couple's overall ability to achieve their treatment goals. However, while empirical evidence supports cognitive-affective-behavioral approaches to dealing with problems and distress in general, evidence supporting their use specifically as part of a treatment plan for PE has not been generated. Whether such issues should be addressed as part of a larger treatment plan is a point of discussion for both the therapist and the couple.

> **Cognitive-affective strategies used in combination with behavioral strategies are likely to enhance treatment outcomes**

Parameters Affecting Treatment

Depending on the level of PE severity, the goals described above could typically be achieved in just a couple of sessions; however, if significant relationship issues and partner dysfunction exist, substantially more sessions may be required. These procedures may also help the couple de-emphasize the focus on intercourse and orgasm within the sexual relationship and may help reduce the man's performance anxiety, which, because it presumably operates through sympathetic pathways, may prime the ejaculatory response prematurely. Ideally, as the man and his partner develop a greater sense of self-efficacy, reliance on oral medications or topical crèmes, if they are used adjunctively, can be reduced.

Dealing with Resistance. Some patients seeking counseling for PE or other sexual problems exhibit various forms of "resistance" to the traditional behavioral approaches. Levine (1992) posits five sources for this resistance:
- when the PE and associated problems maintain a sexual equilibrium and cover up the female partner's sexual disorder or concerns;
- when the individual or couple has unrealistic expectations about sexual performance;
- when there are major relationship problems;
- when male or female partner deceit is present; and
- when PE is the consequence of a major health problem.

In addition, given the increasing attention to emerging biological solutions for sexual problems, some patients insist only on taking the "right pill," and resist exploring cognitive/behavioral and relationship issues.

> **Men with PE may come to therapy with negative coping strategies from attempting to deal with the problem on their own**

Related to the concept of treatment resistance is the issue of "home remedies." Prior to treatment, men with PE may adopt negative coping strategies that actually worsen the condition (e.g., Wincze & Carey, 1991); that is, the attempted solutions become more of a source of difficulty than the initial issue (Hackney & Cormier, 1995). For example, as pointed out previously, most PE men assume that paying *less* attention to the sexual stimuli by actively distracting themselves will help control their ejaculation. Yet, this strategy decreases the awareness of the sexual sensations of the ejaculatory response needed to gain greater control and reduces the enjoyment of the orgasm, due to increased anxiety and focus on sexual performance.

Many couples report that an exclusive focus on the duration and quality of intercourse directly contradicts a healthy focus on developing a mutually satisfying sexual life. Indeed, a strong focus on coitus is counterproductive, particularly since many men without PE ejaculate within 2 min of intromission, and a sizable percentage of women achieve orgasm through direct clitoral stimulation rather than through intercourse (Wincze & Carey, 1991).

Psychosexual Approaches: Relationship

Relationship issues are generally inseparable from cognitive-affective-behavioral issues, but they deserve special mention (see Rowland, 2011). As with other psychosexual approaches, couples therapy may have only minimal impact on ejaculatory latency. Yet, relationship issues are likely to figure heavily in sexual dysfunctions, particularly ones such as PE where one or both partners are sexually dissatisfied or frustrated (Revicki et al., 2008; Rosen & Althof, 2008; Rowland et al., 1998). To this point, it is noteworthy that partners of men with PE report much higher levels of interpersonal difficulty compared with partners of men who do not have this disorder (Patrick et al., 2005).

Higher levels of interpersonal difficulty have been reported by partners of men with PE compared to partners of men without PE

Men with PE may also feel that they are "letting their partners down" and believe that their relationship would improve if they did not have PE. The partners themselves are more prone to sexual problems, as rates of female sexual dysfunction (difficulty becoming aroused and reaching orgasm) and sexual dissatisfaction have been shown to be higher when the male partner has PE.

Promoting effective communication is a relationship therapy technique used for couples with PE

Given the above, it is generally agreed that including the partner in the treatment of PE has greater potential to produce rapid and substantial therapeutic change. For example, to improve long-term outcomes, cognitive and sexual therapy approaches rely on effective communication between the man and his partner, including all aspects of sexual interaction, whether functional or dysfunctional. Besides more effective communication for the PE couple, use of other relationship therapy techniques including reframing, symptom prescription, use of paradox, and giving directives may be productive in alleviating PE. Close monitoring by the therapist of both benefits and negative reactions resulting from couple interactions during therapy sessions is essential. Communication skills training for the couple using the PLISSIT framework (see Table 8), along with other relationship-oriented techniques, may improve overall sexual satisfaction and may be best accomplished by in-session practice and by outside-of-session practice with noncoital sex.

Pharmacological Treatment

Not so long ago, treatment options for PE were limited primarily to behavioral approaches. The past 2 decades have seen an increasing use of pharmaceutical treatments for PE, which have typically taken one of two forms: anesthetizing ointments or crèmes applied to the penis that attenuate penile sensitivity, and orally based neurotransmitter reuptake inhibitors – especially SSRIs – that act primarily by affecting central serotonergic activity (see Table 10).

Table 10
Common Biomedical Treatments for Premature Ejaculation[a]

Treatment	Class	Route	Common trade name	Daily (D) or on-demand (OD)	Effective rating	Side effects
Clomipramine	Tricyclic	Oral	Anafranil	D, OD	+++	☹☹☹
Paroxetine	SSRI	Oral	Paxil	D	+++	☹☹
Sertraline	SSRI	Oral	Zoloft	D	++	☹☹
Fluoxetine	SSRI	Oral	Prozac	D	++	☹☹
Citalopram	SSRI	Oral	Celexa	D	+	☹☹
Dapoxetine	SSRI	Oral	Priligy	OD	++	☹
Lidocaine Prilocaine	Anesthetic	Topical	---	OD	++	☹

Note. [a]Most drugs are used off-label in the treatment of premature ejaculation. Dapoxetine has been approved for the treatment of premature ejaculation by regulatory agencies in various parts of the world.

Because of the economic incentives attached to the development and use of pharmacological agents, both classes of agents – ointments and oral drugs – have been studied quite extensively, with most studies using a double-blind placebo-controlled design; and both classes have been shown to be quite effective in delaying the ejaculatory response. Table 10 provides a list of common pharmacological agents that have been used to increase ejaculatory latency.

Topical Ointments, Crèmes, Gels, and Sprays

Topical ointments, crèmes, gels, and sprays used here are local anesthetics that diminish sensation in the sensory organ, in this case the penis. These preparations typically contain lidocaine, prilocaine, or both, and may more than double the ejaculatory latency for men with PE, as well as increase reported ejaculatory control and quality of life (e.g., Dinsmore et al., 2007). The major downside, although preventable by using a condom, is attenuated vaginal sensitivity and female anorgasmia. However, this group of treatment options often provides an expedient and inexpensive means to increase the ejaculatory latency in men with PE.

Topical ointments, crèmes, gels, and sprays diminish sensation in the penis in order to increase ejaculatory latency

Neurotransmitter Reuptake Inhibitors

This class of medications has been shown to have varying effects on delaying the ejaculatory response. Several points of information are relevant to understanding the treatment of PE with oral pharmaceuticals.

- *Treatment regimens.* The use of pharmacological agents for the treatment of PE has most often involved daily dosing. A number of recent studies, however, have attempted to demonstrate that on-demand use of these agents can also be effective; that is, taking the drug several hours prior to anticipated sexual activity will also delay ejaculation.

SSRIs such as citalopram, fluoxetine, fluvoxamine, paroxetine, sertraline, and clomipramine are used off-label in the treatment of PE

- *SSRIs*, known most for their antidepressant use, include five compounds, all of which have similar pharmacological action: citalopram, fluoxetine, fluvoxamine, paroxetine, and sertraline. Paroxetine appears to be the most effective compound, typically delaying ejaculatory response somewhere between several minutes to more than 5 min. None of these compounds has received regulatory agency (e.g., US Food and Drug Administration [FDA]) approval, although they have been prescribed off-label for the treatment of PE, typically at lower doses than when used as an antidepressant. Most are given as a daily treatment, but fluoxetine, sertraline, and paroxetine appear to be effective when given as a single dose 4–6 hr prior to intercourse (McMahon et al., 2004; Rowland et al., 2010).

- *Clomipramine* was among the first antidepressants used to delay ejaculation. This drug is a tricyclic antidepressant that affects not just serotonin, but also dopamine and norepinephrine uptake. Presumably, the serotonergic action is responsible for the effect on ejaculation. Clomipramine, like the SSRIs, is used off-label in the treatment of PE and is effective both with daily and on-demand dosing, but because of the stronger adverse effects, its use has waned somewhat over the years (Strassberg, de Gouveia Brazao, Rowland, Tan, & Slob, 1999).

- *Dapoxetine* is the first compound developed specifically for the treatment of PE. This drug also acts as an uptake inhibitor (like the SSRIs) and, given its other pharmacokinetics (rapid onset and short half-life), is designed to be taken on demand 1–2 hr prior to intercourse, and increases the latency to ejaculation from about 1 to several minutes (Pryor et al., 2006). Although dapoxetine has been approved for use in a number of European and Asian countries, it has not been approved by the US FDA.

- *Treatment of PE and comorbid erectile dysfunction* may also be attempted by combining antiejaculatory and proerectile drugs. About one third of men with PE also report problems with erection, and in these instances it is important to determine which problem is primary and which is secondary. For example, if a man is ejaculating quickly in order to avoid losing an erection, then the erectile problem needs to be addressed. In some instances, PE and ED are concomitant, with no clear etiological sequence, and these men may be candidates for treatment with both an SSRI and a PDE-5 inhibitor such as sildenafil (Viagra). Because SSRIs themselves can exacerbate an erectile problem and therefore the man may not respond well to an SSRI by itself, the addition of a PDE-5 inhibitor helps the man maintain his erection and reduce performance anxiety while delaying his ejaculation (Sommer, Klotz, & Mathers, 2005).

Mechanism of Action

SSRIs are hypothesized to work by inhibiting the serotonergic trigger for ejaculation

These drugs, basically SSRIs or variants, presumably work by inhibiting the central (brain or upper spinal cord) serotonergic trigger for ejaculation. Men with PE have been hypothesized to have hyposensitivity of 5-HT_{2C} and/or hypersensitivity of 5-HT_{1A} receptors, and therefore agents that affect activity at these receptors presumably increase the ejaculatory threshold. In blocking the reuptake of serotonin (5-HT) from the synaptic cleft, more serotonin remains available for synaptic transmission which then inhibits the ejaculatory process. The process is, of course, significantly more complex, as long-term use of a pharmacological agent such as an SSRI may induce changes in presynaptic and postsynaptic receptor sites and receptor sensitivity, which modulate synaptic activity even further, in some instances perhaps even reducing synaptic transmission. Whether the SSRIs truly delay ejaculation through their action on serotonergic systems involved in the ejaculatory response has not been directly demonstrated in men, although the hypothesis is plausible. Furthermore, the site of action of these drugs, whether in the brain, spinal cord, or both, is unknown.

Efficacy, Prognosis, and Problems

Overall efficacy for some of the above pharmacological agents is robust. Most men report longer latencies to ejaculation, a sense of being able to delay their ejaculation, and improved overall sexual satisfaction when using these agents.

The primary disadvantages of oral medications for PE include (1) the symptomatic approach to treatment – relapse occurs in the absence of drug use as men do not develop better control over their ejaculatory response when they are not taking the drug – and (2) the fact that, as with any drug, unwanted side effects occur (although most are fairly well tolerated). Perhaps because of these disadvantages, adherence to daily dosing regimens is not high, reportedly only around 50%, and this is problematic for couples who may have intercourse several times weekly or less. As data accrue, on-demand use will undoubtedly show higher adherence.

> **Disadvantages of treatment with pharmacological agents include its focus on symptoms and its adverse side effects**

4.3.5　Combinations of Methods

The severity of the PE may suggest varied treatment approaches that combine oral medications and stimulus reduction crèmes (applied to the penis) with either brief or more extended cognitive-behavioral counseling. As with ED, these pharmacological strategies can assist in redeveloping self-confidence and self-efficacy and afford the man the opportunity to develop and use cognitive-behavioral strategies as his response latency approximates a more typical pattern. These strategies may be acquired through bibliotherapy, but the patient and his partner can also benefit from a counselor who can educate them about the sexual response cycle, facilitate communication about sexual issues, and give permission regarding an expanded repertoire of behaviors for greater sexual satisfaction.

> **A combination of cognitive-behavioral counseling and drug treatment may produce the best long-term results**

Based on the above rationale and assumptions, combining behavioral therapy with drug treatment has thus been advocated as a method of treating PE because such therapeutic strategies develop better communication skills among couples, increase adherence to medication, and help couples set realistic goals regarding relationship and sexual satisfaction (Althof, 2006b). Nevertheless, this approach, while plausible and logical, has been supported by only a handful of randomized, controlled clinical studies (Melnik, Glina, Rodrigues, 2009; Rowland, Cooper, & Macias, 2008). For example, one recent open-label study evaluated the addition of sildenafil to paroxetine treatment in conjunction with psychological and behavioral counseling. Men with PE who had failed other treatments found that the combination of drug treatment and psychosexual counseling improved ejaculatory latencies (Chen, Mabjeesh, Matzkin, & Greenstein, 2003). In general, however, combination treatment might be expected to have a more durable effect because the psychosexual counseling component facilitates long-term behavioral changes (e.g., learning methods to control the timing of ejaculation) and improves sexual self-confidence (Althof, 2006a; Althof, 2006b; Perelman, 2006a; Rowland et al., 2008).

4.4   Treatment of Delayed and Inhibited Ejaculation

4.4.1   Nomenclature and Definition

Of all the male sexual dysfunctions, inhibited or retarded ejaculation is the least common, least studied, and least understood. This dysfunction typically results in a lack of sexual fulfillment for both the man and his partner, and men whose sexual relationships are disrupted because of their inability to ejaculate and reach orgasm experience a number of psychological consequences, including anxiety, distress, and lack of confidence. Such negative effects are likely to be compounded when a couple hopes that intercourse will lead to pregnancy.

The terms *retarded ejaculation, delayed ejaculation, inadequate ejaculation, inhibited ejaculation, idiopathic anejaculation, primary impotentia ejaculations,* and *psychogenic anejaculation* have all been used synonymously to describe a delay or absence of male orgasmic response. As with the term *premature ejaculation,* the terminology most commonly used, *retarded ejaculation,* is sometimes avoided because of its pejorative association. However, no consensus currently exists with respect to terminology within the clinical/ biomedical community. Sometimes these dysfunctions, along with other related problems such as a decrease in ejaculatory volume or force, are collectively referred to as male orgasmic disorders (MODs), but this nomenclature lacks specificity. So for this discussion, any problem related to difficulty reaching orgasm/ejaculation has been subsumed under the general nomenclature of *inhibited ejaculation* or *IE*. Although it makes sense to distinguish "delayed" ejaculation – usually referring to the occurrence of ejaculation, but only after a prolonged period of time – from "inhibited" ejaculation – a condition in which ejaculation seldom or never occurs – this distinction is more useful for purposes of etiology; it is generally not relevant with respect to treatment.

The DSM-IV-TR defines IE as the persistent or recurrent delay in, or absence of, orgasm after a normal sexual excitement phase during sexual activity that the clinician, taking into account the person's age, judges to be adequate in focus, intensity, and duration. The disturbance causes marked distress or interpersonal difficulty; it should not be better accounted for by another Axis I disorder or caused exclusively by the direct physiological effects of a substance or a general medical condition (American Psychiatric Association, 2000). Similarly, the World Health Organization Second Consultation on Sexual Dysfunction defines IE as the persistent or recurrent difficulty, delay in, or absence of attaining orgasm after sufficient sexual stimulation, which causes personal distress (McMahon et al., 2004).

There are no clear operationalized criteria as to when a man actually meets the conditions for IE, but, taken together, the following criteria help guide the clinician in an IE diagnosis:

- *Absence or delay of ejaculation.* Given that most sexually functional men ejaculate within about 7–10 min following intromission (Patrick et al., 2005), a clinician might assume that men with latencies beyond 20 or 30 min (and who experience consequent distress) or men who simply cease sexual activity due to exhaustion or irritation qualify for this diagnosis.
- *Inability to shorten the latency to ejaculation.*

> **Inhibited ejaculation typically leads to a lack of sexual fulfillment for the man and his partner**

> **IE is characterized by persistent or recurrent difficulty, delay in, or absence of orgasm after sufficient sexual stimulation**

- *Distress, bother, or some other negative consequence* that results from the absence or delay of ejaculation. The fact that a man and his partner seek help for the problem is usually sufficient evidence for this third IE criterion. In some instances, the treatment driver may be one of procreation, but men distressed by their inability to achieve orgasm in response to manual, oral, or vaginal stimulation by their partner are likely to seek treatment as well.

Failure to reach ejaculation can be a lifelong condition ("primary," *e.g.*, congenital anorgasmia) or an acquired or secondary problem. It can occur with every sexual encounter, or it may be intermittent or situational. Normative descriptive data from large samples of IE men have not been available, but a recent analysis (Perelman, 2004) identified 25% of a clinical sample suffering from primary IE, with the remainder reporting that IE was a secondary problem. Some men with secondary IE can masturbate to orgasm, whereas others, for multiple reasons, will not or cannot (e.g., due to religious or cultural sanctions). Loss of masturbatory capacity secondary to emotional or physical trauma is also seen. Approximately 75% of one sample (Perelman, 2004) could reach orgasm through masturbation, while the remainder either would not or could not.

Men with IE sometimes have little or no difficulty attaining or keeping their erections

As with men with other types of sexual dysfunction, men with IE typically indicate relationship distress, sexual dissatisfaction, anxiety about their sexual performance, and larger health issues – significantly higher than sexually functional men. In addition, along with other sexually dysfunctional counterparts, men with IE typically report lower frequencies of coital activity (Rowland, van Diest, Incrocci, & Slob, 2005). A distinguishing characteristic of men with IE – and one that has implications for treatment – is that they usually have little or no difficulty attaining or keeping their erections – in fact they are often able to maintain erections for prolonged periods of time. But despite their good erections, they report low levels of subjective sexual arousal, at least compared with sexually functional men (Rowland, Keeney, & Slob, 2004).

4.4.2   Prevalence

IE is less common and less studied than other male sexual dysfunctions

The prevalence of delayed and/or inhibited ejaculation is unclear, partly because of the dearth of normative data for defining the duration of "normal" ejaculatory latency, particularly regarding the right tail of the distribution (i.e., beyond the mean latency to orgasm). Furthermore, larger epidemiological studies have not subdivided various types of ejaculatory problems (e.g., delayed versus inhibited versus diminished ejaculatory function), raising further questions regarding the validity of published prevalence data. In general, IE has been reported at low rates in the literature, rarely exceeding 3% (Laumann et al., 1999; Perelman et al., 2004; Simons & Carey, 2001). Since the beginning of sex therapy, IE was seen as a clinical rarity, with Masters and Johnson (1970) initially reporting only 17 cases. Apfelbaum (2000) reported 34 cases and Kaplan (1995) fewer than 50 cases in their respective practices. Other, more recent population-based surveys have suggested percentages from 5% to 11%, depending on the duration of the dysfunction (Laumann et al., 1999; Lewis et al., 2010, Richardson & Goldmeier, 2006). However, based on clinical experiences, some urologists and sex therapists suspect an increasing incidence of IE (Perelman, 2003a; Perelman et al., 2004; Simons & Carey, 2001), particularly in view of the aging population in Western societies. Specifically, as men age, ejaculatory function as a whole tends to diminish, possibly accounting for a perceived increase in the prevalence of IE.

4.4.3   Etiology, Risk Factors, and Comorbidities

In some instances, a somatic condition may account for IE, and indeed, any procedure or disease that disrupts sympathetic or somatic innervation to the genital region has the potential to affect ejaculatory function and orgasm. Thus, spinal cord injury, multiple sclerosis, pelvic-region surgery, severe diabetes, and medications that inhibit α-adrenergic innervation of the ejaculatory system have been associated with IE (Master & Turek, 2001; Vale, 1999; Witt & Grantmyre, 1993). Nevertheless, a sizable portion of men with IE exhibit no clear somatic factors that account for the disorder. As the result of their inability to ejaculate, these men also do not experience orgasm. Men whose problem cannot be linked to a specific somatic or pathophysiological etiology are frequently assumed, though perhaps in error, to have a psychogenic etiology. Just as a pathophysiological etiology should not be assumed without a thorough medical investigation, a psychogenic etiology should not be assumed without an appropriate psychosexual history. Of course, psychogenic and biogenic etiologies are neither independent nor mutually exclusive classifications – not only do the categories themselves overlap (e.g., is a problem of diminished sympathetic arousal a psychogenic or biogenic classification?), but the causes of sexual dysfunctions often include a mix of factors involving both domains. In fact, recent empirical studies suggest that IE is unlikely to result from a single set of causal factors.

> A psychogenic etiology for IE should not be assumed without an appropriate psychosexual history

Biological Factors

The precise mechanism of ejaculation is much less firmly established than the physiology of erection, and for this reason, the physiology of ejaculatory disorders is less understood than that of ED. For conceptual convenience, normal ejaculation is identified by its two seamless phases, emission and expulsion, with each representing distinct events regulated by separate neural pathways (Shafik, 1998). After a variable period of sensory stimulation and psychosexual arousal, a rapid, involuntary sequence of events ensues (Masters & Johnson, 1966; Motofei & Rowland, 2005a). The emission phase, under the control of the sympathetic nervous system, begins with closure of the bladder neck to prevent urinary contamination followed by deposition of semen from the seminal vesicles and prostate into the posterior urethra. A sensation of "ejaculatory inevitability" arises from the urethral distension, which, in turn, stimulates rhythmic contractions of the bulbocavernous and ischiocavernous muscles responsible for semen expulsion – a process under probable parasympathetic control (Motofei & Rowland, 2005b).

The ejaculatory reflex is mediated through the spinal control center, sometimes also referred to as the spinal ejaculation generator, spinal pattern generator, or spinal pacemaker. A combination of sensory input from the pudendal nerve (dorsal nerve of the penis) and descending cerebral pathways activates the spinal ejaculation generator, which coordinates the sympathetic, parasympathetic, and motor outflow needed to induce emission and expulsion (Motofei & Rowland, 2005a; Perelman et al., 2004). As with other spinal reflex processes (e.g., urination), cerebral control is presumed to supersede spinal control of the ejaculatory response (Motofei & Rowland, 2005a).

As one attempts to understand biogenic causes of ejaculatory dysfunction, it is essential to distinguish those factors that are physiological from those that are pathophysiological. *Physiological* refers to those that are biologically inherent to the system, perhaps "hardwired" through genetic and normal maturational processes. *Pathophysiological* refers to those that are medical and occur through disruption of the normal physiological processes, through disease, trauma, surgery, medication, and so on. Pathophysiological causes of IE are far more readily identifiable; they generally surface during a medical history and examination, and they typically stem from fairly predictable sources: anomalous anatomic, neuropathic, endocrine, and medication (iatrogenic). For example, surgical therapy for prostatic obstruction is likely to disrupt bladder neck competence during emission. Pathological lesions of the sympathetic innervation of the coordinated ejaculatory reflex may have variable effects on the quality of ejaculation or orgasm. All types of IE show an age-related increase in prevalence, and there is also concomitant increased severity with lower urinary tract symptoms independent of age (Blanker et al., 2001; Rosen et al., 2003). Commonly used medications (see Summary Box), particularly antidepressants, may centrally inhibit or delay ejaculation as well. A comprehensive list of such pharmacological agents may be found in recent reviews (e.g., Perelman et al., 2004).

Examples of Classes of Pharmacological Agents That May Delay Ejaculation

Antihypertensives

Thiazide diuretics

Tricyclic and SSRI antidepressants

Tranquilizers and antipsychotics

Muscle relaxants

Alcohol, hypnotics, and sedatives

There is an important distinction between physiological and pathophysiological causes, the latter of which are more easily identified

More difficult to identify are inherent physiological factors that account for variation in ejaculatory latency and thus might play a role in IE (particularly primary anorgasmia).The distribution of ejaculatory latency is best represented as a positively skewed distribution (see Figure 2), with some men consistently ejaculating rapidly and others consistently ejaculating only after longer periods of stimulation. This tendency toward shorter or longer ejaculatory latencies is more than likely influenced by inherent biological mechanisms. However, the specific mechanisms responsible for such variation are unknown. Low penile sensitivity, most often associated with aging (Paick et al., 1998; Rowland, 1998), may exacerbate difficulty with reaching orgasm, but it is unlikely to be a primary cause. Alternatively, variability in the sensitivity of the ejaculatory reflex may be a factor, as several studies have demonstrated shorter latencies and stronger bulbocavernous electromyography and event-related potential responses in men with premature ejaculation – perhaps men with IE exhibit long-latency and weaker electromyography and event-related potential patterns respectively. More likely, however, ejaculatory response and latency are influenced by central (cognitive-affective-arousal) processes than dominated exclusively by the hardwiring of the spinal reflex components (Motofei & Rowland, 2005a). That is, key to understanding any ejaculatory disorder (either premature or retarded ejaculation) is understanding the factors that account for variation in latency to ejaculation following vaginal intromission. As with many biobehavioral responses, variation in ejaculatory latency is undoubtedly under the control of both biological and psychobehavioral factors. And while the ejaculatory latency range for each individual may be biologically set or predisposed (e.g., via "hardwired" genetic factors), the actual timing or moment of ejaculation within that range depends on a variety of contextual, psychobehavioral, and relationship-partner variables. Such thinking is clearly supported by the fact that ejaculatory latency in men with ejaculatory disorders (either premature or retarded ejaculation) is often quite different during coitus than during masturbation (Rowland, DeGouvea Brazao, Strassberg, & Slob, 2000).

Variation in ejaculatory latency is controlled by both biological and psychological-behavioral factors

Psychogenic Factors

Multiple psychosocial explanations have been offered for IE, with unconscious aggression, unexpressed anger, and malingering recurring as themes in the psychoanalytic literature. In addition, pregnancy fears were emphasized for a while, as professional referral was often tied to the female partner's wish to conceive. Masters and Johnson (1970) were the first to suggest an association between IE and religious orthodoxy, positing that certain beliefs may inhibit normal ejaculatory function or limit the sexual experience necessary for developing ejaculatory response. Consistent with this notion, a recent report of a clinical sample of 75 men with IE (Perelman, 2004) noted about 35% scored high on religious orthodoxy. Some of these men tended to have limited sexual knowledge and had masturbated minimally or not at all. Others, similar to their more secular counterparts, had masturbated for years, but with guilt and anxiety about their behavior (Perelman, 2003a).

Although religious orthodoxy may play a role in IE for some men, the majority of men do not fall into this category. A number of relevant behavioral, psychological, and relationship factors appear to contribute to difficulty reaching orgasm for these men (Table 11). For example, men with IE sometimes indicate greater arousal and enjoyment from masturbation than from intercourse. Interestingly, correlational evidence suggests that masturbatory frequency may be one predisposing factor for IE, since a portion of men who present with coital IE typically report high levels of masturbatory activity.

Men with IE may indicate greater arousal and enjoyment from masturbation than from intercourse

This "autosexual" orientation may involve an idiosyncratic and vigorous masturbation style – carried out with high frequency – which does not "match" vaginal stimulation. Apfelbaum (2000) labels this as a desire disorder specific to "partnered sex." Specifically, men with IE engage in self-stimulation that is stereotypical in speed, pressure, duration, and intensity necessary to produce an orgasm, and often different from what they might experience with a partner

Table 11
Factors to Consider in the Diagnosis of Men With Inhibited Ejaculation

Biological
Medications
Age
Disease or trauma in pelvic area or lower urinary tract
Insufficient penile stimulation

Psychobehavioral
Diminished subjective sexual arousal
Autoerotic (masturbation) orientation
Anxiety about performance
Sexual fantasies not aligned with reality
Sexual/genital pain
Sociocultural and religious beliefs and attitudes

Relationship
Sexual dysfunction in partner
Partner considered unattractive
Excessive desire to please partner

(Perelman, 2004). Thus, they may predispose themselves to difficulty with a partner and experience secondary IE. Consistent with this idea, recent evidence indicates that, unlike sexually functional men or men with other sexual dysfunctions, men with IE report *better* erections during masturbation than during foreplay or intercourse (Rowland et al., 2005).

Disparity between the reality of sex with the partner and the sexual fantasy (whether or not unconventional) used during masturbation is another potential cause of IE (Perelman, 1994; Perelman & Rowland, 2006). This disparity involves many factors, such as partner attractiveness and body type, sexual orientation, and the specific sex activity performed. In summary, high-frequency idiosyncratic masturbation, combined with fantasy/partner disparity, may well predispose men to experiencing problems with arousal and ejaculation.

IE may be more of a problem with psychosexual arousal than with ejaculatory response

The above patterns suggest that IE men, rather than withholding ejaculation, as had been suggested by earlier psychoanalytic interpretations, may lack sufficient levels of psychosexual arousal during coitus to achieve orgasm. That is, their arousal response to their partner cannot match their response to self-stimulation and self-generated fantasy. In this respect, IE may be viewed more as a problem of psychosexual arousal than a problem of the ejaculatory response. Support for this idea has been provided by several observations. First, psychophysiological investigation of men with IE has demonstrated that although these men attain erectile responses comparable to sexually functional controls or men with PE during visual and penile psychosexual stimulation, they report far lower levels of subjective sexual arousal (Rowland et al., 2004; Rowland et al., 2005). Second, Apfelbaum (2000) has suggested that the couple interprets the man's strong erectile response as erroneous evidence that he is ready for sex and capable of achieving orgasm. Consistent with this line of thinking, inadequate arousal may be responsible for increased anecdotal clinical reports of IE for men using oral medications for the treatment for ED (Perelman, 2003a). Specifically, men using PDE-5 inhibitors (such as Cialis or Viagra) experience restored erections, but are unaware that having a usable erection does not ensure that adequate psychoemotional arousal has been achieved. In other words, some men may not experience sufficient erotic stimulation before and during coitus to reach orgasm; they think their erect state is an indication of sexual arousal when it primarily indicates only a medication-induced vasocongestive response (Perelman & Rowland, 2006).

Finally, the evaluative/performance aspect of sex with a partner often creates "sexual performance anxiety" for the man, a factor that may contribute to IE. Such anxiety typically stems from the man's lack of confidence to perform adequately, to appear and feel attractive (body image), to satisfy his partner sexually, and to experience an overall sense of self-efficacy (Althof et al., 2004; Zilbergeld, 1993). The impact of this anxiety on men's sexual response varies depending on the individual and the situation. But in some men, it may interfere with the ability to respond adequately, and it may, as a result, generate a number of maladaptive responses (e.g., setting unrealistic expectations). With respect to IE, anxiety surrounding the inability to ejaculate may draw the man's attention away from erotic cues that normally serve to enhance arousal. Apfelbaum (2000), for example, has emphasized the need to remove the "demand" (and thus anxiety-producing) characteristics of the situation, noting that men with IE may be overconscientious about pleasing their partner. This ejaculatory performance anxiety interferes with the erotic sensations of genital stimulation, resulting in levels of sexual excitement and arousal that are insufficient for climax (although more than adequate to maintain their erections).

> Men with IE may exhibit "ejaculatory performance" anxiety that can interfere with their ability to reach orgasm

4.4.4 Evaluation

The diagnostic evaluation of IE focuses on finding potential physical and specific psychological/learned causes of the disorder (see Table 11). A genitourinary examination and medical history may identify physical anomalies associated with ejaculatory dysfunction. In addition, concomitant or contributory neurological, endocrinological, or erectile disorders can be identified and addressed. Particular attention should be given to identifying reversible urethral, prostatic, epididymal, and testicular infections.

A focused psychosexual evaluation – important even to a diagnosis that is primarily pathophysiological – is critical for men with no obvious somatic etiology. Evaluation typically begins by differentiating this sexual dysfunction from other sexual problems (e.g., terminating intercourse due to pain) and reviewing the conditions under which the man is able to ejaculate, (e.g., during sleep, with masturbation, with partner's hand or mouth stimulation, or, though infrequently, with varying coital positions). Domains related to the psychological and relationship issues commonly associated with IE (identified in the previous section) require investigation. Thus, the developmental course of the problem – including predisposing issues of religiosity – and variables that improve or worsen performance, particularly those related to psychosexual arousal, should be noted. Coital and masturbatory patterns, perceived partner attractiveness, the use of fantasy during sex, and anxiety surrounding performance all require exploration. If orgasmic attainment had previously been

> Evaluation should include an exploration of the developmental course of the problem

possible, the clinician should review the life events/circumstances temporally related to orgasmic cessation – events in question may be pharmaceuticals, illness, or a variety of life stressors and other psychological factors previously highlighted in the section on etiology. Generally, a complete evaluation should identify all possible predisposing, precipitating, and maintaining factors for the dysfunction.

Since many men attempt their own remedies, the patient's previous approaches to improving ejaculatory response should be investigated, including the use of herbal or folk therapies, prior treatments, and home remedies (e.g., using particular cognitive or behavioral strategies). Information regarding the partner's perception of the problem and satisfaction with the overall relationship is often helpful. Once this body of knowledge is complete, an appropriate treatment plan, developed in conjunction with the couple, can be implemented. In summary, appropriate assessment requires an appreciation of the interdependent influence of biological, psychological, and relationship factors on arousal and ejaculatory function.

4.4.5   Methods of Treatment

Treatment strategies for IE may be conceptualized as increasing the level of sexual arousal so the man is able to surpass the ejaculatory threshold; this process most often benefits from cooperation of the sexual partner. Discussion of a potential biological predisposition is often helpful in reducing patient and partner anxiety and mutual recriminations, while simultaneously assisting the formation of a therapeutic alliance with the clinician (Rowland et al., 2005). In general, treatment may include one or more of the following approaches:

- Psychobehavioral
  - Masturbatory training for increasing arousal
  - Integration with partner pleasuring and activity
- Pharmacological

Psychobehavioral Approaches

Masturbatory Training and Retraining

Goal of most therapeutic techniques for IE is to stimulate higher levels of psychosexual arousal to enable orgasm in partnered experience

Masters and Johnson (1970) were among the first to advocate specific exercises as part of the treatment for IE. Current sex therapy approaches continue to emphasize the importance of masturbation in the treatment of IE; however, much of the focus now is on masturbatory *re*training integrated into sex therapy (Apfelbaum, 2000; Perelman; 2004; Sank, 1998). As characterized by Perelman, masturbation serves as a type of "dress rehearsal" for sex with a partner. By informing the patient that his difficulty is merely a reflection of "not rehearsing the part he intended to play," the stigma associated with this problem can be minimized, and cooperation of both the patient and partner can be evoked. Of course, masturbation retraining is only a means to an end, and the goal of most current therapeutic techniques for IE (either primary or secondary IE) is not merely to provide more intense stimulation, but rather to stimulate higher levels of psychosexual arousal and, eventually, orgasm within the framework of a satisfying experience.

Primary IE. Men with primary IE who do not have a clear pathophysiological etiology, like their female counterparts, typically need help in determining their sexual arousal preferences through self-exploration and stimulation. Masturbation training may use a modification of the model described by Barbach (1974) for women, although for men the use of vibrators is usually unnecessary (Perelman, 2007). Progressing from neutral sensations to the ability to identify and experience pleasurable sensations is encouraged, but this need not be aimed at achieving orgasm, at least initially.

Typically, self-stimulation techniques incorporating fantasy can be used to achieve incremental increases in arousal. Fantasy can help block inhibiting thoughts – often a critical step that might otherwise result in interference with the progression of sexual arousal. An important component in the treatment of any type of IE is the removal of "demand" or "performance" anxiety (Apfelbaum, 2000). To reduce anxiety, IE treatment may include recognition of men's overeagerness to please their partners, validation of (though not necessarily encouragement of) the man's autosexual orientation, removal of stigmas suggesting hostility or withholding toward their partner, and general anxiety reduction techniques such as relaxation and desensitization. Finally, the man is taught to effectively communicate his preferences to his partner so that both their needs are incorporated into the sexual experience.

Secondary IE and the Management of Resistance. Therapy for secondary IE follows a strategy similar to that of primary IE. However, the clinician or urologist may counsel these patients to suspend masturbatory activity and limit orgasmic release to only the desired activity, which is typically coitus. Advice to temporarily reduce and/or discontinue masturbation for any length of time (e.g., 14–60 days) may be met with significant resistance by the patient. As a result, the clinician will need to provide strong support and encouragement to the patient to ensure that he adheres to this suspension. In addition to suspending masturbation, during coitus the patient should be encouraged to use fantasy and bodily movements, which help approximate the thoughts and sensations previously experienced in masturbation. Resistance is minimized and the success of the process enhanced when the partner is supported by the clinician and understands that the alteration in coital style consists of temporary, successive steps to reaching a long-term goal of mutual coital harmony and satisfaction.

Sometimes the issue of masturbation suspension must be compromised and negotiated with the patient. A man who continues to masturbate, for example, may be encouraged to alter the style of masturbation ("switch hands") and to approximate (in terms of speed, pressure, and technique) the stimulation likely to be experienced through manual, oral, or vaginal stimulation by his partner (Perelman, 2006b).

Partner Involvement and Issues

To increase satisfactory outcomes from treatment, the partner needs to cooperate with the therapeutic process, finding ways to pleasure the man that enhance arousal and that can be incorporated into the couple's lovemaking. Sexual fantasies may have to be realigned so that thoughts experienced during masturbation better match those occurring during coitus. Efforts to increase the attractiveness and seductive/arousing capacity of the partner and thus to reduce

A man's partner can cooperate by finding ways to pleasure him that enhance arousal and can be incorporated into lovemaking

the disparity between the fantasy and actuality may be useful, as significant disparity tends to characterize more severe and recalcitrant IE and relationship problems, with a consequent poorer treatment prognosis (Perelman, 2001a, 2001b).

Addressing the total level of stimulation includes consideration of both physiological and psychological processes

Schnarch (1988) has proposed a reformulation of the human sexual response cycle, primarily for the treatment of ED, which emphasizes the interactive or relational nature, as opposed to the common compartmentalization and polarization, of the physiological and psychological components of sexual functioning (see Osborne & Rowland, 2007). This model also has relevance to the treatment of IE. The model proposes assessing *total stimulus level* – defined as the sum of both physiological/tactile stimulation and psychological or emotional/relational processes – in relation to the patient's threshold levels for genital vasocongestive responses associated with arousal and orgasm. This model considers both the quality and quantity of the patient's and his partner's behaviors that provide *physical stimulation*, as well as the physiological factors that influence the body's capacity to "transmit" the stimulation (negatively, aging or the presence of an interfering medical condition). The model also examines the *psychological processes* that either support or interfere with stimulus transmission, such as the individual's ability to attend to sensation, the impact of anxiety, and the relational or interactive patterns that influence response. Both in assessment and in planning treatment, this model challenges the clinician to consider both physiological and psychological processes and to recognize that intervention in either or both domains may be necessary to maximize the total level of stimulation and the patient's capacity to reach arousal or ejaculatory thresholds (Milsten & Slowinski, 1999; Schnarch, 1988). Only when clinicians assess both processes can they accurately determine the extent to which interventions in either or both domains may be restorative.

Relational/behavioral interventions that alter sexual *style* and expand the sexual *repertoire* have the potential of compensating for the reduced physiological potential that naturally occurs with age or with a medical condition. The total level of stimulation reflects the combination of both physiological and psychological stimulation, and interventions can take place at either or both levels to maximize the patient's potential for reaching the threshold level of arousal needed for adequate erectile and ejaculatory response. With age, for example, the need for increasing levels of stimulation to reach arousal and orgasmic threshold occurs naturally. At the same time, the total level of transmitted stimulation often decreases due to illness, poor technique, limited repertoire, sexual boredom, decreasing levels of intimacy, performance anxiety, or other psychological or relational processes.

While a number of other partner-related issues may affect a man's ejaculatory response, two deserve special attention: conception/procreation and anger/resentment (Perelman & Rowland, 2006). Regarding conception (assuming a female partner), the pressure of the woman's "biological clock" is often the initial treatment driver for IE. If the clinician suspects the patient's IE is related to fear of conception, he may inquire about the patient's ability to experience coital ejaculation using contraception (including condoms) but not during "unprotected" sex. If the patient's fears are confirmed, the therapist must refocus the treatment, at least temporarily, on the underlying issues responsible for the man's concerns. Resolving this issue typically requires individual consultations with the man and occasionally with the partner.

As IE treatment progresses, interventions may be experienced as mechanistic and insensitive to the partner's needs and goals. In particular, many partners respond negatively to the impression that the man is essentially masturbating himself with his partner's various body parts, distinct from engaging in the type of connected lovemaking the partner may prefer (Perelman & Rowland, 2006). This perception is exacerbated when men need actual pornography/erotica rather than mere fantasy to distract themselves from negative thoughts and emotions in order to function sexually. Indeed, because these men are often quite disconnected emotionally from their partners, the clinician must help the partner become comfortable with the idea of postponing gratification of her or his needs. Once the patient has progressed to a level of functionality, the clinician can then encourage greater sensitivity on the man's part.

Pharmacological Approaches

In contrast with the array of pharmacological treatments available to men with other sexual dysfunctions, safe and effective pharmacological treatments for decreasing ejaculatory latency have not been identified for general medical use. Perhaps the most common reason for considering a pharmacological approach lies in an IE condition that is *initially* induced pharmacologically through the use of prescription medications.

Pharmacologically induced IE may sometimes be treated by replacing the initial medication with an approved one with a lower side effect. For example, a patient treated with SSRI antidepressants such as fluoxetine may be switched to other antidepressants such as bupropion, nefazodone, or buspirone (see McMahon et al., 2004; Rowland et al., 2010). Although these antidepressants also may have serotonergic action, they appear to have less impact on ejaculatory function. In instances where a medication has ejaculatory-inhibiting effects (e.g., beta blockers, antipsychotics, etc.), the choices are fewer and less attractive. In such instances, in consultation with the physician, a discussion regarding the reduction of the dosage or an occasional drug holiday should be considered.

Finally, although not approved by regulatory agencies for the treatment of IE, the antiserotonergic agent cyproheptadine and the dopamine agonist amantadine have been used with moderate success in patients with IE (McMahon et al., 2004). However, the lack of large, controlled studies with these and other ejaculatory-facilitating agents suggests a high ratio of adverse effects to potential efficacy. Furthermore, a lack of efficacy in men with IE may result, in part, from the potentially strong psychological and relational contributions to this dysfunction. Nevertheless, as research continues to uncover greater understanding of the ejaculatory process, the likelihood of finding proejaculatory agents increases.

> Safe and effective pharmacological treatments for decreasing ejaculatory latency have not been identified for general medical use

4.4.6 Treatment Efficacy

Despite the lack of an easily identified etiology for IE, the lack of rigorous testing of methodologies, and anecdotal assumptions as a difficult-to-treat problem, reported success rates for the treatment of IE *not* due to pathophysiological origin have been reasonably high, ranging from 40% to over 80% (e.g., McMahon et al., 2004; Munjack & Kanno, 1979; Perelman, 2003a). Confidence in such reports, however, is limited by the few studies that have been conducted, their uncontrolled designs (including lack of placebo groups), the lack of standardized treatment formulations, and the heterogeneous samples that include men with conditions with varying biological and psychological etiologies.

While sex therapists typically provide treatment for IE, family physicians or urologists may use psychosexual therapeutic strategies described herein

The treatment for IE described herein would typically be conducted by a therapist rather than a urologist or general practitioner. However, depending on comfort level, preference, resources, and availability, the urologist may choose to refer the man to a sex therapist or counselor colleague or to treat the man with IE him/herself (Perelman, 2003b). Indeed, regarding this last possibility, urologists and other health care providers could readily incorporate some of the psychosexual therapeutic strategies mentioned here into a short counseling/guidance/education session within the framework of an office visit.

5

Final Thoughts and Notes

5.1   Overarching Strategies

Although each sexual problem described in this book may have a different etiology, run a different course, and require a different treatment strategy, a general framework and common approaches can be applied to all men's sexual problems. Even more broadly, many of the therapeutic strategies applied within a *general* counseling framework can be applied to the treatment of sexual problems. The following section reviews a number of fundamental points for the generalist therapist to keep in mind as he or she approaches the treatment of a man with a sexual problem.

5.2   Eleven Pointers From Clinical Notes

(1) *Most people, especially men, have difficulty talking about their sexual problems*, so it is often incumbent upon the therapist to create an atmosphere of comfort and openness. The therapist should support the patient's attempts to communicate concerns related to his sexual life.

(2) *Most therapy for sexual problems need not be extensive.* The therapist should point out to the couple the value of exploring a number of different strategies for achieving higher sexual satisfaction and reassure the patient that these can often be achieved through a limited number of sessions.

(3) *The typical male patient has little or no concept of the sexual response cycle* as understood by clinicians and often noted in textbooks. The therapist should discuss the problems with the patient in familiar language while concomitantly using this conversation to specify the precise nature of the problem – for example, is the problem one of low desire? Of inadequate arousal? Of the inability to keep an erection because of premature ejaculation?

(4) *Men often focus heavily on their genital response.* The therapist should broaden the conversation to include the man's individual experience of the problem, his partner's perspective, general relationship concerns, and other dimensions beyond just the physical.

(5) *Setting clear treatment goals is important for both the patient and the therapist.* The therapist should work with the patient (and partner) to set realistic goals as well as, when appropriate, ones that extend beyond basic "sexual performance" issues.

(6) *An understanding of the physiological, psychological, relational, and sociocultural contribution to the sexual problem is warranted.* The therapist should explore each of these domains at least briefly to determine whether deeper issues need to be addressed.

(7) *Medical issues should be investigated.* The therapist should refer the patient to a physician for a checkup, with advance notation about the sexual problem. A sexual problem is sometimes a manifestation of a larger health issue.

(8) *Communication between partners is important to sexual, partner, and relationship satisfaction.* The therapist should encourage the inclusion of the partner in conversations about therapeutic goals and strategies as well as in the treatment process itself.

(9) *Good coping strategies*, including reframing negative thoughts into positive ones and channeling emotional energy into positive outcomes, *are important elements in dealing with any life problem.* The therapist can apply similar cognitive-affective-behavioral objectives within the context of psychosexual counseling.

(10) *A variety of effective psychological, behavioral, and pharmacological tools are currently available for the treatment of men's sexual problems.* The therapist should select from among those that are both efficacious and acceptable to the patient. While knowing the etiology of the problem is helpful, it may not always dictate all aspects of the treatment strategy. For example, no matter the origin of a sexual problem, the combination of psychosexual and pharmacological strategies often provides an optimal solution.

(11) *Patients will relapse and experience frustration.* The therapist should prepare the patient for relapses and provide periodic follow-up to ensure a high level of treatment satisfaction.

6

Case Vignette

The Situation

Robert and Amy met in law school and were married 2 years after graduating. Both wanted and expected to have fulfilling careers and both initially secured full-time jobs in the same metropolitan corridor. During their courtship and early years of marriage, they enjoyed their new life together, feeling optimistic about their future and emotionally connected – at this time they reported having sex regularly two or three times a week. Robert indicated that he would have liked more frequent sex but did not want to "push" Amy. Amy, for her part, was content with this level of activity and was aware that Robert sometimes masturbated in the intervals between coitus.

Several years later, as the luster of their new relationship began to wear off and as their professional lives demanded more time, long commutes, and sometimes significant travel for one or the other, they settled into a pattern of sex once or twice a week – usually at least one of those instances occurred on the weekend.

Five years into their marriage, Amy, now 34, became pregnant – although the pregnancy was not really planned, it was not unwelcome by either of them. The pregnancy was mildly complicated, and when their daughter Kristin was born, she had a number of health issues that required more than the usual watchful care – for example, she awoke often in the middle of the night, making for many sleepless nights for both parents. To simplify things, Robert and Amy together decided that Kristin should sleep in their room, occasionally in their bed. At this time, Robert and Amy were having sex about once a week or less, typically on the weekend when Kristin was napping. Both enjoyed the sex, although it was often hurried and allowed minimal postcoital time for intimacy. Then when Kristin was 2, Amy decided to leave her full-time job and work part-time so as to spend more time raising their daughter. Kristin continued to sleep in her parents' bed off and on.

It was around this time, when Robert was 37, that he first felt he was having some difficulty getting and keeping an erection. Unconcerned at first, Robert attributed the problem to the stress of his career, heavier now that he was the primary breadwinner. However, as the problem wore on and gradually worsened, Robert was sometimes privately relieved by the stress of his work, by the fact that Amy seemed so focused on their child, and by their busy schedules – they provided convenient excuses to avoid sex. Amy, interpreting that Robert appeared no longer interested in her, began to feel hurt and resentful – the latter because she had felt that she sacrificed her career for their family and now was no longer perceived as an attractive partner. Robert, increasingly concerned about his sexuality, had a one-night stand with a colleague while on a business trip. The sex was awkward and somewhat labored, but Robert was mildly reassured that "sexually, he could still do it."

About 1 year later, now both in their early 40s, in the midst of a heated argument, Robert let out that he had been unfaithful. Amy was devastated and withdrew emotionally and sexually – their sex, which had already become infrequent (about two to three times a month) and somewhat disconnected, ceased altogether. It was at this time that Robert began to masturbate frequently – several times a week. But more devastating, it was shortly after this time that Amy learned she had breast cancer.

The cancer had the effect of drawing them together emotionally, at least for a time, and Robert became supportive and sympathetic. The burden was heavy for both of them – Amy, who always had been very independent, felt that she had become a burden to her family and felt that her very identity as a woman was under attack; and Robert, who became partial caretaker for Amy, assumed much of the care for Kristin while continuing to rise in his law organization as partner. Amy eventually had a full mastectomy and opted against having reconstructive breast surgery, despite mild pressure from Robert. However, with the cancer in remission, Robert and Amy felt they could move on with their lives.

Amy, her reproductive functioning returning and now feeling the pressure of her biological clock, expressed her desire to have a second child. She also saw it as an attempt to retain some of the intimacy that they had regained during her bout with cancer – she felt the emotional closeness might also regenerate sexual interest and passion. Robert, unsure of his own feeling in this regard, verbally went along with Amy's wish, but felt little sexual desire and worried about whether he would be able to perform sexually. Indeed, when Amy indicated it was "time," Robert either could not keep his erection or could not reach orgasm to ejaculation. He turned to a physician for help, and as part of the routine checkup, Robert learned that his blood pressure was significantly elevated. The physician prescribed antihypertensive medication, initially making the erection problem worse, and then upon a follow-up visit prescribed a PDE-5 inhibitor (e.g., Viagra). In the subsequent weeks, Robert reported that he felt more confident about getting and keeping an erection.

However, after several more tries for impregnation, once again the couple began to drift apart emotionally. Amy was sad that she had already lost so much and disappointed that Robert did not appear to share the value of having a second child as evidenced by the fact that he would not deliver, and Robert, feeling little sexual attraction to Amy, feeling that his heroic efforts during Amy's cancer had not been rewarded with breast reconstruction, and already anxious about his erections, was inwardly angered by this new and added expectation.

Although they discussed separation and divorce, their lives were very intertwined by this time and their marriage did have elements of a comfortable routine. Furthermore, both were concerned what effect a divorce might have on Kristin, now 8. At the suggestion of a friend, they decided to seek professional help to see what they could do to mend their marital and sexual relationship.

Clinical Notes and Strategies

This case represents the level of complexity often surrounding a sexual problem. Specifically, the problem encompasses elements of sexual interest/desire, erection problems, and arousal and ejaculation. From an integrative perspective, a mix of somatic/biogenic factors (e.g., hypertension and antihypertensives) combine with psychological (general stressors, anxiety, and lack of confidence) and relationship factors (e.g., issues of control, commitment, attraction, expectation, etc.) to attenuate sexual response.

The psychosexual counseling (in this situation to include the partner) might progress through four general phases:

Phase I: Identifying issues and setting goals, 1–2 sessions
The following issues might be explored in an initial session or two

Medical history, referral to physician of checkup, including cardiovascular check.
Discussion of effects of various medications on sexual response.
Brief psychosexual history, relationship history.
Exploration of components of sexual response: desire/interest, arousal, erection, and ejaculatory response.
Determination of issues that are primary and those that are secondary. For example, is the inhibited ejaculation due to insufficient arousal?
Establishing issues beyond basic sexual response having potential to improve sexual and relationship functioning.
Setting goals for the treatment outcomes.

Phase II: Assessing broad domains of biopsychosocial risk factors, 3–4 sessions
Preliminary steps

Psychoeducation about sexual response, as needed.
Development of communication skills.
Development of the therapist–client relationship and trust.
Individual sessions with each partner – psychological (cognitive-affective), sociocultural factors, etc.
Connection of somatic issues (hypertension, breast cancer) to emotional, sexual, and relationship issues.
Deep exploration of relationship issues in couples format (commitment, control, sacrifice, expectation, etc.).
Connection of relationship issues to sexual issues.

Phase III: Progressive strategies for change and improvement, 2–3 sessions
Continuation of relationship reconstruction through joint activities, etc.

Consideration of behavioral strategies (sensate focus, relaxation, etc.); restrictions on intercourse and masturbation.
Progressive development from sensual to sexual: reclaiming foreplay, attraction, lust, and intimacy.
Dealing with the man's performance issues: Pharmacological augmentation; Cognitive-affective strategies; Dealing with any partner issues.
Revisiting relationship issues: mutual support from partners in reestablishing trust, sexual responsiveness, and intimacy.

Phase IV: Assessment and longer term strategies to sustain improvement, 1–2 sessions

Ongoing support for positive relationship system changes

Reassessment of each phase of the sexual response cycle.

Identification of sexual and relationship areas that continue to need improvement and significant effort.

Reinforce effective communication skills.

Re-strategize use of pharmaceuticals to serve primarily as "back-up."

Prepare couple for relapse and/or regression.

Schedule follow up "booster" session.

7

Further Reading and Resources

Carey, M. P. (1998). Cognitive-behavioral treatment of sexual dysfunction. In V. E. Caballo (Ed.), *International handbook of cognitive and behavioural treatments for psychological disorders* (pp. 251–280). Oxford, UK: Pergamon/Elsevier Science.

This chapter summarizes the application of cognitive-behavioral strategies to situations involving sexual dysfunction. Embedded in a larger volume dealing specifically with cognitive-behavioral approaches toward a variety of specific disorders, therapists who are familiar with CBT will appreciate the application to sexual problems.

Leiblum, S. R. (Ed.). (2007). *Principles and practice of sex therapy.* New York: Guilford Press.

This comprehensive guide may serve as a resource to assess and treat the major female and male sexual dysfunctions. Effective methods for integrating psychological, interpersonal, and medical interventions are demonstrated by leading professionals, along with clinical examples to illustrate the process of therapy and the factors that influence treatment outcomes.

Lue, T. F., Basson, R., Rosen, R., Giuliano, F., Khoury, S., & Montrosi, F. (Eds.). (2004). *Sexual medicine: Sexual dysfunctions in men and women* (pp. 73–116). Paris, France: Health Publications.

This book, geared toward physicians and urologists, provides a good medical perspective on sexual problems. Special topics include brain imaging, expanded information on both male and female sexual dysfunction, quantitative research as opposed to evidence-based medicine, and several psychosexual assessment questionnaires. It presents a relevant viewpoint given that an increasing number of men is seeking treatment through their primary health care providers.

Metz, M., & McCarthy, B. (2003). *Coping with premature ejaculation: How to overcome PE, please your partner, & have great sex.* Oakland, CA: New Harbinger.

This compilation of current, bio-psychologically based, multifaceted methods for overcoming premature ejaculation provides a comprehensive approach for both therapist and, because of its user-friendly nature, clients and their partners. It includes a section to dispel the myths of male sexual performance, a section describing a complete relapse prevention program, and a section discussing the various types of premature ejaculation and ways to identify each.

Osborne, C., & Rowland, D. L. (2007). Psychological factors in male sexual dysfunction. In F. Kandeel (Ed.), *Male sexual dysfunction: Pathophysiology and treatment* (pp. 147–154). New York: Informa Healthcare.

In this chapter the rationale and process for carrying out a psychological evaluation on men seeking help for a sexual problem are outlined. Details are provided on psychosexual and psychological evaluation using both standardized and nonstandardized assessment procedures that can augment the clinician's insight into potential psychological factors impacting the client's sexual functioning.

Porst, H., & Buvat, J. (Eds.). (2006). *Standard practice in sexual medicine.* Malden, MA: Blackwell.

This international guide and reference provides comprehensive coverage of the wide range of diagnostic and treatment options available for both male and female sexual dysfunctions. More medical in its approach, it is useful for identifying symptoms to diagnose and treat sexual disorders and dysfunctions. Treating problems from a urological perspective, the information is often well-integrated with other urological issues. The guide also provides helpful information on the latest developments in pharmacologic approaches.

Rowland, D. L., & Incrocci, L. (Eds.). (2008). *Handbook of sexual and gender identity disorders.* Hoboken, NJ: Wiley.

Written to benefit mental health professionals and primary care physicians, this volume brings together notable experts in the field who provide an interdisciplinary perspective on the description, assessment, and management of sexual dysfunctions in men and women. Including review and treatment of gender identity disorders as well as paraphilias it can serve as a broad reference volume for practitioners.

8

References

Abraham, L., Symonds, T., & Morris, M. F. (2008). Psychometric validation of a sexual quality of life questionnaire for use in men with premature ejaculation or erectile dysfunction. *Journal of Sexual Medicine, 5*(3), 595–601.

Ahn, T., Park, J., Lee, S., Hong, J., Park, N., Kim, J., … Hyun, J. (2007). Prevalence and risk factors for erectile dysfunction in Korean men: Results of an epidemiological study. *Journal of Sexual Medicine, 4*(5), 1269–1276.

Althof, S. E. (2006a). Prevalence, characteristics, and implications of premature ejaculation/rapid ejaculation. *Journal of Urology, 175,* 842–848.

Althof, S. E. (2006b). The psychology of premature ejaculation: Therapies and consequences. *Journal of Sexual Medicine, 3*(Suppl 4), 324–331.

Althof, S. E., Abdo, C., Dean, J., Hackett, G., McCabe, M. P., McMahon, C. G., … Tan, H. M. (2010). International Society for Sexual Medicine's guidelines for the diagnosis and treatment of premature ejaculation. *Journal of Sexual Medicine, 7,* 2947–2969.

Althof, S. E., Lieblum, S. R., Chevert-Measson, M., Hartman, U., Levine, M., McCabe, M., … Wirth, M. (2004). Psychological and interpersonal dimensions of sexual function and dysfunction. In T. F. Lue, R. Basson, R. Rosen, F. Giuliano, S. Khoury, & F. Montrosi (Eds.), *Sexual medicine: Sexual dysfunctions in men and women* (pp. 73–116). Paris, France: Health Publications.

Althof, S. E., Raymond, R., Symonds, T., Mundayat, R., May, K., & Abraham, L. (2006). Development and validation of a new questionnaire to assess sexual satisfaction, control, and distress associated with premature ejaculation. *Journal of Sexual Medicine, 3*(3), 465–475.

American Psychiatric Association. (2000). *Diagnostic and statistical manual of mental disorders* (4th ed., text revision). Washington, DC: Author.

Angst, J. (1998). Sexual problems in healthy and depressed persons. *International Clinical Psychopharmacology, 13*(Suppl 6), S1–S4.

Annon, J. S. (1974). *The behavioral treatment of sexual problems: Vol. 1: Brief therapy.* Honolulu, HI: Kapiolani Health Services.

Annon, J. S. (1975). *The behavioral treatment of sexual problems: Vol. 2: Intensive therapy.* Honolulu, HI: Honolulu Enabling Systems.

Apfelbaum, B. (2000). Retarded ejaculation: A much misunderstood syndrome. In S. R. Lieblum & R. C. Rosen (Eds.), *Principles and practice of sex therapy* (3rd ed.; pp. 205–241). New York: Guilford Press.

Aschka, C., Himmel, W., Ittner, E., & Kochen, M. M. (2001). Sexual problems of male patients in family practice. *The Journal of Family Practice, 50,* 773–778.

Baldwin, D. S. (1996). Depression and sexual function. *Journal of Psychopharmacology, 10*(Suppl 1), 30–34.

Bancroft, J. (1989). *Human sexuality and its problems.* Edinburgh, Scotland: Churchill Livingstone.

Bancroft, J., Graham, C. A., Janssen, E., & Sanders, S. A. (2009). The dual control model: Current status and future directions. *Journal of Sex Research, 46*(2–3), 121–142.

Bandura, A. (1977). Self-efficacy: Toward a unifying theory of behavioral change. *Psychological Review, 84*(2), 191–215.

Barbach, L. G. (1974). *For yourself: A guide to female orgasmic response.* New York: Doubleday.

Barnes, T., & Eardley, I. (2007). Premature ejaculation: The scope of the problem. *Journal of Sex and Marital Therapy, 33*(2), 151–170.

Basson, R. (2001). Using a different model for female sexual response to address women's problematic low sexual desire. *Journal of Sex and Marital Therapy, 27,* 395–403.

Blanker, M. H., Bosch, J. L., Groeneveld, F. P., Bohnen, A. M., Prins, A., Thomas, S., & Hop, W. C. (2001). Erectile and ejaculatory dysfunction in a community based sample of men 50 to 78 years old: Prevalence, concern, and relation to sexual activity. *Urology, 57,* 763–768.

Boolel, M., Allen, M. J., Ballard, S. A., Gepi-Attee, S., Muirhead, G. J., Naylor, A. M., ... Gingell, C. (1996). Sildenafil: An orally active type 5 cyclic GMP-specific phosphodiesterase inhibitor for the treatment of penile erectile dysfunction. *International Journal of Impotence Research, 8,* 47–52.

Burnett, A. L. (1999). Neurophysiology of erectile function and dysfunction. In W. J. G. Hellstrom (Ed.), *The handbook of sexual dysfunction* (pp. 12–17). San Francisco, CA: The American Society of Andrology.

Busse, R. T., Kratochwill, T. R., & Elliot, S. N. (1999). Influences of verbal interactions during behavioral consultations on treatment outcomes. *Journal of School Psychology, 37*(2), 117–143.

Byrne, D., & Schulte, L. (1990). Personality dispositions as mediators of sexual responses. *Annual Review of Sex Research, 1,* 93–117.

Cappelleri, J. C., Althof, S. E., O'Leary, M. P., Glina, S., King, R., Stecher, V. J., ... Siegel, R. L. (2007). Clinically meaningful improvement on the self-esteem and relationship questionnaire in men with erectile dysfunction. *Quality of Life Research, 16,* 1203–1210.

Cappelleri, J. C., Althof, S. E., Siegel, R. L., Shpilsky, A., Bell, S. S., & Duttagupta, S. (2004). Development and validation of the Self-Esteem And Relationship (SEAR) questionnaire in erectile dysfunction. *International Journal of Impotence Research, 16*(1), 30–38.

Carey, M. P. (1998). Cognitive-behavioral treatment of sexual dysfunction. In V. E. Caballo (Ed.), *International handbook of cognitive and behavioural treatments for psychological disorders* (pp. 251–280). Oxford, UK: Pergamon/Elsevier Science.

Chen, J., Mabjeesh, N. J., Matzkin, H., & Greenstein, A. (2003). Efficacy of sildenafil as adjuvant therapy to selective serotonin reuptake inhibitor in alleviating premature ejaculation. *Urology, 61,* 197–200.

Clayton, A. H., & Balon, R. (2009). The impact of mental illness and psychotropic medications on sexual functioning: The evidence and management. *Journal of Sexual Medicine, 6,* 1200–1211.

Conaglen, J. V., & Conaglen, H. M. (2009). The effect of treating male hypogonadism on couples' sexual desire and function. *Journal of Sexual Medicine, 6*(2), 456–463.

Conte, H. R. (1986). Multivariate assessment of sexual dysfunction. *Journal of Consulting Clinical Psychology, 54*(2), 149–157.

Cooper, A. J., Cernovsky, Z. Z., & Colussi, K. (1993). Some clinical and psychometric characteristics of primary and secondary premature ejaculators. *Journal of Sex and Marital Therapy, 19*(4), 276–288.

Cooper, S. & Rowland, D. L. (2005). Treatment implications of behavioral and psychological research on premature ejaculation. *Current Sexual Health Reports, 2*(2), 77–81.

Corona, G., Petrone, L., Mannucci, E., Jannini, E. A., Mansani, R., Magini, A., ... Maggi, M. (2004). Psycho-biological correlates of rapid ejaculation in patients attending an andrologic unit for sexual dysfunctions. *European Urology, 46*(5), 615–622.

Corretti, G., Pierucci, S., De Scisciolo, M., & Nisita, C. (2006). Comorbidity between social phobia and premature ejaculation: Study on 242 males affected by sexual disorders. *Journal of Sex and Martial Therapy, 32,* 183–187.

Corty, E. W., Althof, S. E., & Kurit, D. M. (1996). The reliability and validity of a sexual functioning questionnaire. *Journal of Sex and Marital Therapy, 22*(1), 27–34.

Costa, P. T., Jr., Fagan, P., Piedmont, R. L., Ponticas, Y., & Wise, T. N. (1992). The five-factor model of personality and sexual functioning in outpatient men and women. *Psychiatric Medicine, 10,* 199–215.

Davidson, J. M., Kwan, M., & Greenleaf, W. J. (1982). Hormonal replacement and sexuality. *The Journal of Clinical Endocrinology and Metabolism, 11,* 599–623.

Dinsmore, W. W., Hackett, G., Goldmeier, D., Waldinger, M., Dean, J., Wright, P., ... Wyllie, M. (2007). Topical eutectic mixture for premature ejaculation (TEMPE): A novel aerosol-delivery form of lidocaine-prilocaine for treating premature ejaculation. *British Journal of Urology International, 99*(2), 369–375.

Ellis, A. (1992). Group rational-emotive and cognitive-behavioral therapy. *International Journal of Group Psychotherapy, 42*(1), 63–80.

Engel, G. L. (1977). The need for a new medical model: A challenge for biomedicine. *Science, 96,* 129–136.

Everitt, B. J. (1995). Neuroendocrine mechanisms underlying appetitive and consummatory elements of masculine sexual behaviour. In J. Bancroft (Ed.), *The pharmacology of sexual function and dysfunction* (pp. 15–31). Amsterdam, The Netherlands: Exerpta Medica.

Feldman, H. A., Goldstein, I., Hatzichristou, D. G., Krane, R. J., & McKinlay, J. B. (1994). Impotence and its medical and psychosocial correlates: Results of the Massachusetts male aging study. *Journal of Urology, 151,* 54–61.

Fichten, C. S., Spector, I., & Libman, E. (1988). Client attributions for sexual dysfunction. *Journal of Sex and Marital Therapy, 14*(3), 208–224.

Figueira, I., Possidente, E., Marques, C., & Hayes, K. (2001). Sexual dysfunction: A neglected complication of panic disorder and social phobia. *Archives of Sexual Behavior, 30*(4), 369–377.

Gooren, L. (2008). Androgens and endocrine function in aging men: Effects on sexual and general health. In D. L. Rowland & L. Incrocci (Eds.), *Handbook of sexual and gender identity disorders* (pp. 122–153). Hoboken, NJ: Wiley.

Greenberg, L. (2004). Emotion-focused therapy. *Clinical Psychology and Psychotherapy, 11,* 3–16.

Grenier, M. A., & Byers, S. (1995). Rapid ejaculation: A review of conceptual, etiological, and treatment issues. *Archives of Sexual Behavior, 24,* 447–472.

Hackett, G. I. (2008). Disorders of male sexual desire. In D. L. Rowland & L. Incrocci (Eds.), *Handbook of sexual and gender identity disorders* (pp. 5–31). Hoboken, NJ: Wiley.

Hackney, H. E., & Cormier, L. S. (2009). *The professional counselor: A process guide to helping* (6th ed.). Boston, MA: Allyn and Bacon.

Harland, R., & Huws, R. (1997). Sexual problems in diabetes and the role of psychological intervention. *Journal of Sex and Marital Therapy, 12,* 147–157.

Hawton, K. (1985). Sex therapy: A practical guide. Oxford, UK: Oxford University Press.

Hawton, K. (1989). Sexual dysfunctions. In K. Hawton, P. Salkovskis, J. Kirk, & D. Clark (Eds.), *Cognitive behavioral therapy for psychiatric problems* (pp. 370–405). Oxford, UK: Oxford University Press

Hawton, K. (1992). Sex therapy research: Has it withered on the vine. *Annual Review of Sex Research, 3,* 49–72.

Hawton, K. (1998). Integration of treatments for male erectile dysfunction. *Lancet, 351,* 7–8.

Kaplan, H. S. (1974). *The new sex therapy.* New York: Brunner/Mazel.

Kaplan, H. S. (1979). *Disorders of sexual desire and other new concepts and techniques in sex therapy.* New York: Brunner/Mazel.

Kaplan, H. S. (1995). *The evaluation of sexual disorders: Psychological and medical aspects.* New York: Brunner/Mazel.

La Pera, G., & Nicastro, A. (1996). A new treatment for premature ejaculation: The rehabilitation of the pelvic floor. *Journal of Sex and Marital Therapy, 22,* 22–26.

Laumann, E. O., Nicolosi, A., Glasser, D. B., Paik, A., & Gingell, C. (2005). Sexual problems among men and women aged 40–80 yrs: Prevalence and correlates identified in the global study of sexual attitudes and behaviours. *International Journal of Impotence Research, 17,* 39–57.

Laumann, E., Paik, A., & Rosen, R. C. (1999). Sexual dysfunction in the United States: Prevalence and predictors. *Journal of the American Medical Association, 281,* 537–544.

Levine, S. (1992). Helping men to control ejaculation. In S. Levine (Ed.), *Sexual life: A clinician's guide* (pp. 90–106). New York: Plenum.

Lewis, R. W., Fugl-Meyer, K. S., Bosch, R., Fugl-Meyer, A. R., Laumann, E. O., Lizza, E., & Martin-Morales, A. (2004). Definitions, classification, and epidemiology of sexual dysfunction. In T. F. Lue, R. Basson, R. Rosen, F. Giuliano, S. Khoury, & F. Montrosi (Eds.), *Sexual medicine: Sexual dysfunctions in men and women* (pp. 37–72). Paris, France: Health Publications.

Lewis, R. W., Fugl-Meyer, K. S., Corona, G., Hayes, R. D., Laumann, E. O., Moreira, E. D., Jr., ... Segraves, T. (2010). Definitions/epidemiology/risk factors for sexual dysfunction. *Journal of Sexual Medicine, 7,* 1598–1607.

Lewis, R. W., Yuan, J., & Wang, R. (2008). Male sexual arousal disorder. In D. L. Rowland & L. Incrocci (Eds.), *Handbook of sexual and gender identity disorders* (pp. 32–67). Hoboken, NJ: Wiley.

Lilleleht, E., & Leiblum, S. R. (1993). Schizophrenia and sexuality: A critical review of the literature. *Annual Review of Sex Research, 4,* 247–276.

Loeb, T. B., Williams, J. K., Carmona, J. V., Rivkin, I., Wyatt, G. E., Chin, D., & Asuan-O'Brien, A. (2002). Child sexual abuse: Associations with the sexual functioning of adolescents and adults. *Annual Review of Sex Research, 13,* 307–345.

LoPiccolo, J. (1999). Psychological assessment of erectile dysfunction. In C. Carson, R. Kirby, & I. Goldstein (Eds.), *Textbook of erectile dysfunction* (pp. 183–193). Oxford, UK: ISIA Medical Media.

Lue, T. F. (1992). Physiology of erection and pathophysiology of impotence. In P. C. Walsh, A. B. Retik, T. A. Stamey, & E. D. Vaughan Jr. (Eds.), *Campbell's urology* (pp. 709–728). Philadelphia, PA: W. B. Saunders Company.

Madakasira, S., & St. Lawrence, J. (1997). Premature ejaculation: assessment and treatment. *Bailliere's Clinical Psychiatry, 3,* 91–112.

Marks, I. M. (1981). Review of behavioral psychotherapy: Part II: Sexual disorders. *The American Journal of Psychiatry, 138,* 750–756.

Master, V. A., & Turek, P. J. (2001). Ejaculatory physiology and dysfunctions. *Urologic Clinics of North America, 28,* 363–375.

Masters, W. H., & Johnson, V. E. (1966). Human sexual response. Boston, MA: Little, Brown.

Masters, W. H., & Johnson, V. E. (1970). Human sexual inadequacy. Boston, MA: Little, Brown.

Maurice, W. L. (2007). Sexual desire disorders in men. In S. R. Lieblum (Ed.), *Principles and practice of sex therapy* (pp. 181–211). New York: Guildford Press.

McCabe, M. P. (1997). Intimacy and quality of life among sexually dysfunctional men and women. *Journal of Sex and Marital Therapy, 23,* 276–290.

McMahon, C. G. (2002). Long term results of treatment of premature ejaculation with selective serotonin re-uptake inhibitors. *International Journal of Impotence Research, 14*(Suppl. 3), S19.

McMahon, C. G., Abdo, C., Incrocci, L., Perelman, M., Rowland, D. L., Stuckey, B., ... Xin, Z. C. (2004). Disorders of orgasm and ejaculation in men. In Lue, T. F., Basson, R., Rosen, R. C., Giuliano, F., Khoury, S., & Montorsi, F. (Eds.), *Sexual medicine: Sexual dysfunction in men and women* (pp. 409–468). Paris, France: Health Publications.

McMain, S., Pos, S., & Iwakabe, S. (2010). Facilitating emotion regulation: General principles for psychotherapy. *Psychotherapy, 45*(3), 16–21.

McMullin, R. E., & Giles, T. R. (1998). Cognitive-behavioral therapy: A restructuring approach. New York: Grune & Stratton.

Melnik, T., Glina, S., & Rodrigues, O. M., Jr. (2009). Psychological intervention for premature ejaculation. *Nature Reviews Urology, 6,* 501–508.

Metz, M., Pryor, J., Nescavil, L., Abuzzahab, F., & Koznar, J. (1997). Premature ejaculation: A psychophysiological review. *Journal of Sex and Marital Therapy, 23,* 3–23.

Michetti, P. M., Rossi, R., Bonanno, D., De Dominicis, C., Iorl, F., & Simonelli, C. (2007). Dysregulation of emotions and premature ejaculation (PE): Alexithymia in 100 outpatients. *Journal of Sexual Medicine, 4*(5), 1462–1467.

Milsten, R., & Slowinski, J. (1999). *The sexual male: Problems and solutions.* New York: W. W. Norton.

Moreira, E. D., Jr. (2005). Help-seeking behaviour for sexual problems: The global study of sexual attitudes and behaviors. *International Journal of Clinical Practice, 59,* 6–16.

Motofei, I., & Rowland, D. L. (2005a). Neurophysiology of the ejaculatory process: Developing perspectives. *British Journal of Urology International, 96*(9), 1333–1338.

Motofei, I., & Rowland, D. L. (2005b). The physiological basis of human sexual arousal: Neuroendocrine sexual asymmetry. *International Journal of Andrology, 28*(2), 78–87.

Munjack, D. J., & Kanno, P. H. (1979). Retarded ejaculation: A review. *Archives of Sexual Behavior, 8,* 139–150.

Munjack, D. J., Kanno, P. H., & Oziel, L. J. (1978). Ejaculatory disorders: Some psychometric data. *Psychological Reports, 43*(3), 783–787.

Nobre, P. J., & Pinto-Gouveia, J. (2009). Questionnaire of cognitive schema activation in sexual context: A measure to assess cognitive schemas activated in unsuccessful sexual situations. *Journal of Sex Research, 46*(5), 425–437.

Osborne, C., & Rowland, D. L. (2007). Psychological factors in male sexual dysfunction. In F. Kandeel (Ed.), *Male sexual dysfunction: Pathophysiology and treatment* (pp. 147–154). New York: Informa Healthcare.

Paick, J. S., Jeong, H., & Park, M. S. (1998). Penile sensitivity in men with early ejaculation. *International Journal of Impotence Research, 10,* 247–250.

Palmore, E. B. (1985). How to live longer and like it. *Journal of Applied Gerontology, 4,* 1–8.

Patrick, D. L., Althof, S. E., Pryor, J. L., Rosen, R., Rowland, D. L., Ho, K. F., … Jamieson, C. (2005). Premature ejaculation: An observational study of men and their partners. *Journal of Sexual Medicine, 2,* 358–367.

Patrick, D. L., Rowland, D. L., & Rothman, M. (2007). Interrelationships among measures of premature ejaculation: The central role of perceived control. *Journal of Sexual Medicine, 4*(3), 780–788.

Perelman, M. (1994). Masturbation revisited. *Contemporary Urology, 6*(11), 68–70.

Perelman, M. (2001a). Integrating sildenafil and sex therapy: Unconsummated marriage secondary to ED and RE. *Journal of Sex Education and Therapy, 26*(1), 13–21.

Perelman, M. (2001b). Sildenafil, sex therapy, and retarded ejaculation. *Journal of Sex Education and Therapy, 26,* 13–21.

Perelman, M. (2003a). Regarding ejaculation: Delayed and otherwise [Letter]. *Journal of Andrology, 24,* 496.

Perelman, M. (2003b). Sex coaching for physicians: Combination treatment for patient and partner. *International Journal of Impotence Research, 15*(Suppl 5), S67–74.

Perelman, M. (2004). Retarded ejaculation. In J. Mulhull (Ed.), *Current sexual health reports 2004* (pp. 95–101). Philadelphia, PA: Current Science.

Perelman, M. (2006a). A new combination treatment for premature ejaculation: A sex therapist's perspective. *Journal of Sexual Medicine, 3*(6), 1004–1012.

Perelman, M. (2006b). Unveiling retarded ejaculation [Abstract]. *Journal of Urology, 175*(Suppl 4), 430.

Perelman, M. (2007). Combination treatment for retarded ejaculation [Editorial comment on manuscript for article "Assessment of penile vibratory stimulation as a management strategy in men with secondary retarded orgasm" by C. J. Nelson, A. Ahmed, R. Valenzuela, M. Parker, & J. P. Mulhall]. *Urology, 69,* 552–555.

Perelman, M., McMahon, C., & Barada, J. (2004). Evaluation and treatment of the ejaculatory disorders. In T. Lue (Ed.), *Atlas of male sexual dysfunction* (pp. 127–157). Philadelphia, PA: Current Medicine, LLC.

Perelman, M., & Rowland, D. L. (2006). Retarded ejaculation. *World Journal of Urology, 24,* 645–652.

Perelman, M., & Rowland, D. L. (2008). Retarded and inhibited ejaculation. In D. L. Rowland & L. Incrocci (Eds.), *Handbook of sexual and gender identity disorders* (pp. 100–121). Hoboken, NJ: Wiley.

Pfaus, J. G., Kippin, T. E., & Coria-Avila, G. (2003). What can animal models tell us about human sexual response. *Annual Review of Sex Research, 14,* 1–63.

Porst, H., Gilbert, C., Collins, S., Huang, X., Symonds, T., Stecher, V., & Hvidsten, K. (2007). Development and validation of the Quality of Erection Questionnaire. *Journal of Sexual Medicine, 4,* 372–381.

Porst, H., Montorsi, F., Rosen, R. C., Gaynor, L., Grupe, S., & Alexander, J. (2007). The Premature Ejaculation Prevalence and Attitudes (PEPA) survey: Prevalence, comorbidities, and professional help-seeking. *European Urology, 51,* 816–824.

Pridal, C. G., & LoPiccolo, J. (2000). Multi-element treatment of desire disorders: Integration of cognitive, behavioral, and systemic therapy. In S. R. Lieblum & R. C. Rosen (Eds.), *Principles and practice of sex therapy* (pp. 205–241). New York: Guilford Press.

Prochaska, J. O., & Norcross, J. C. (2007). *Systems of psychotherapy: A transtheoretical approach* (6th ed.). Pacific Grove, CA: Brooks/Cole.

Pryor, J. L., Althof, S. E., Steidle, C., Rosen, R. C., Hellstrom, W. J., Shabsigh, R., ... Kell, S. (2006). Efficacy and tolerability of dapoxetine in treatment of premature ejaculation: An integrated analysis of two double-blind, randomized controlled trials. *Lancet, 368*(9539), 929–937.

Ragin, D. F. (2011). *Health psychology: An interdisciplinary approach to health.* Upper Saddle River, NJ: Pearson Education Company/Prentice Hall.

Revicki, D., Howard, K., Hanlon J, Mannix, S., Greene, A., & Rothman, M. (2008). Characterizing the burden of premature ejaculation from a patient and partner perspective: A multi-country qualitative analysis. *Health and Quality of Life Outcomes, 6,* 33.

Richardson, D., & Goldmeier, D. (2006). Recommendations for the management of retarded ejaculation: BASHH Special Interest Group for Sexual Dysfunction. *International Journal of STD and AIDS, 17,* 7–13.

Riley, A., & Riley, E. (2005). Premature ejaculation: presentation and associations: An audit of patients attending a sexual problems clinic. *International Journal of Clinical Practice, 59,* 1482–1487.

Rosen, R. C., & Althof, S. (2008). Impact of premature ejaculation: The psychological, quality of life, and sexual relationship consequences. *Journal of Sexual Medicine, 5,* 1296–1307.

Rosen, R. C., Altwein, J., Boyle, P., Kirby, R. S., Lukacs, B., Meuleman, E., ... Giuliano, F., (2003). Lower urinary tract symptoms and male sexual dysfunction: The Multinational Survey of the Aging Male (MSAM-7). *European Urology, 44,* 637–649.

Rosen, R. C., Cappelleri, J. C., & Gendrano, N., III. (2002). The International Index of Erectile Function (IIEF): A state-of-the-science review. *International Journal of Impotence Research, 14,* 226–244.

Rosen, R. C., Cappelleri, J. C., Smith, M. D., Lipsky, J., & Pena, B. M. (1999). Development and evaluation of an abridged, 5-item version of the international index of erectile function (IIEF-5) as a diagnostic tool for erectile dysfunction. *International Journal of Impotence Research, 11,* 319–326.

Rosen, R. C., Catania, J., Pollack, L., Althof, S., O'Leary, M., & Seftel, A. (2004a). Male Sexual Health Questionnaire (MSHQ): Scale development and psychometric validation. *Journal of Urology, 64*(4), 777–782.

Rosen, R. C., Hatzichristou, D., Broderick, G., Clayton, A., Cuzin, B., Derogatis, L., ... Seftel, A. (2004b). Clinical evaluation and symptom scales: Sexual dysfunction assessment in men. In T. F. Lue, R. Basson, R. Rosen, F. Giuliano, S. Khoury, & F. Montrosi (Eds.), *Sexual medicine: Sexual dysfunctions in men and women* (pp. 173–220). Paris, France: Health Publications.

Rowland, D. L. (1998). Penile sensitivity in men: An overview of recent findings. *Urology, 52,* 1101–1105.

Rowland D. L. (2007) Sexual health and problems: Erectile dysfunction, premature ejaculation, and orgasmic disorders. In J. Grant & M. Potenza (Eds.), *Textbook of men's mental health* (pp. 171–204). Arlington, VA: American Psychiatric Association Press.

Rowland, D. L. (2010). Genital and heart rate response to erotic stimulation in men with and without premature ejaculation. *International Journal of Impotence Research, 22,* 318–324.

Rowland, D. L. (2011). Psychological impact of premature ejaculation and barriers to its recognition and treatment. *Current Medical Research and Opinion, 27*(8), 1509–1518.

Rowland, D. L., & Burnett, A. (2000). Pharmacotherapy in the treatment of male sexual dysfunction. *Journal of Sex Research, 37,* 226–243.

Rowland, D. L., & Cooper, S. E. (2005). Behavioral and psychological models in ejaculatory function research. *Current Sexual Health Reports, 2*(1), 29–34.

Rowland, D. L., & Cooper, S. E. (2011). Practical tips for sexual counseling and psychotherapy in premature ejaculation. *Journal of Sexual Medicine, 8,* 342–352.

Rowland, D. L., Cooper, S. E., & Macias, L. (2008). Pharmaceutical companies could serve their own interests by supporting research on the efficacy of psychotherapy on premature ejaculation. *International Journal of Impotence Research, 20,* 115–120.

Rowland, D. L., Cooper, S. E., & Slob, A. K. (1998). The treatment of premature ejaculation: Psychological and biological strategies. *Drugs of Today (Barc), 34*(10),879–899.

Rowland, D. L., & Crawford, S. B. (2011). Idiosyncratic heart rate response in men during sexual arousal. *Journal of Sexual Medicine, 8*(5), 1383–1389.

Rowland, D. L., DeGouvea Brazao, C., Strassberg, D. A., & Slob, A. K. (2000). Ejaculatory latency and control in men with premature ejaculation: A detailed analysis across sexual activities using multiple sources of information. *Journal of Psychosomatic Research, 48,* 69–77.

Rowland, D. L., Keeney, C., & Slob, A. K. (2004). Sexual response in men with inhibited or retarded ejaculation. *International Journal of Impotence Research, 16,* 270–274.

Rowland, D. L., McMahon C. G., Abdo, C., Chen, J., Jannini, E., Waldinger, M. D., & Ahn, T. (2010). Disorders of orgasm and ejaculation in men. *Journal of Sexual Medicine, 7,* 1668–1686.

Rowland, D. L., Patrick, D. L., Rothman, M., & Gagnon, D. D. (2007). The psychological burden of premature ejaculation. *Journal of Urology, 177*(3), 1065–1070.

Rowland, D. L., Perelman, M. A., Althof, S. E., Barada, J., McCullough, A., Bull, S., ... Ho, K. (2004). Self-reported premature ejaculation and aspects of sexual functioning and satisfaction. *Journal of Sexual Medicine, 1*(2), 225–232.

Rowland, D. L., & Slob, A. K. (1992). Vibrotactile stimulation enhances sexual arousal in sexually functional men: a study using concomitant measures of erection. *Archives of Sexual Behavior, 21,* 387–400.

Rowland, D. L., & Slob, A. K. (1997). Premature ejaculation: Psychophysiological considerations in theory, research, and treatment. *Annual Review of Sex Research, 8,* 224–253.

Rowland, D. L., Tai, W. L., Slob, A. K. (2003). An exploration of emotional response to erotic stimulation in men with premature ejaculation: Effects of treatment with clomipramine. *Archives of Sexual Behavior, 32*(2), 145–153.

Rowland, D. L., van Diest, S., Incrocci, L., & Slob, A. (2005). Psychosexual factors that differentiate men with inhibited ejaculation from men with no dysfunction or another sexual dysfunction. *Journal of Sexual Medicine, 2*(3), 383–389.

Rust, J., & Golombok, S. (1986). *The Golombok Rust Inventory of Sexual Satisfaction.* Odessa, FL: Psychological Assessment Resources.

Sank, L. I. (1998). Traumatic masturbatory syndrome. *Journal of Sex and Marital Therapy, 24,* 37–42.

Scepkowski, L. A., Wiegel, M., Bach, A. K., Weisberg, R. B., Brown, T. A., & Barlow, D. H. (2004). Attributions for sexual situations in men with and without erectile disorder: Evidence from a sex-specific attributional style measure. *Archives of Sexual Behavior, 33*(6), 559–569.

Schnarch, D. M. (1988). Talking to patients about sex: Part II. *Medical Aspects of Human Sexuality, 22,* 97–106.

Schnarch, D. M. (1991). *Constructing the sexual crucible: An integration of sexual and marital therapy.* New York: W. W. Norton.

Schnarch, D. M. (2000). Desire problems: A systemic perspective. In S. R. Lieblum & R. C. Rosen (Eds.), *Principles and practice of sex therapy* (pp. 17–56). New York: Guilford Press.

Schover, L. R., Friedman, J. M., Weiler, S. J., Heiman, J. R., & LoPiccolo, J. (1982). Multiaxial problem-oriented system for sexual dysfunctions: An alternative to DSM-III. *Archives of General Psychiatry, 39,* 614–619.

Schreiner-Engel, P., & Schiavi, R. C. (1986). Lifetime psychopathology in individuals with low sexual desire. *The Journal of Nervous and Mental Disease, 174,* 646–651.

Selvin, E., Burnett, A. L., & Platz, E. A. (2007). Prevalence and risk factors for erectile dysfunction in the US. *The American Journal of Medicine, 120*(2), 151–157.

Semans, J. (1956). Premature ejaculation. *Southern Medical Journal, 49,* 352–358.

Shafik, A. (1998). The mechanisms of ejaculation: The glans-vasal and urethromuscular reflexes. *Archives of Andrology, 41,* 71–78.

Simons, J., & Carey, M. P. (2001). Prevalence of sexual dysfunctions: Results from a decade of research. *Archives of Sexual Behavior, 30*(2), 177–219.

Sommer, F., Klotz, T., & Mathers, M. J. (2005). Treatment of premature ejaculation: A comparative vardenafil and SSRI crossover study [Abstract]. *Journal of Urology, 173*(4), 202.

Spanier, G. B. (1976). Measuring dyadic adjustment: New scales for assessing the quality of marriage and similar dyads. *Journal of Marriage and Family, 38,* 15–28.

Spector, I. P., & Carey, M. P. (1990). Incidence and prevalence of the sexual dysfunctions: A critical review of the empirical literature. *Archives of Sexual Behavior, 19,* 389–403.

Sternberg, R. J., & Barnes, M. (1988). *The psychology of love.* New Haven, CT: Yale University Press.

Strassberg, D. S., de Gouveia Brazao, C. A., Rowland, D. L., Tan, P., & Slob, A. K. (1999). Clomipramine in the treatment of rapid (premature) ejaculation. *Journal of Sex and Marital Therapy, 25*(2), 89–101.

Symonds, T., Perelman, M., Althof, S., Giuliano, F., Martin, M., Abraham, L, … May, K. (2007a). Further evidence of the reliability and validity of the premature ejaculation diagnostic tool. *International Journal of Impotence Research, 19*(5), 521–525.

Symonds, T., Perelman, M. A., Althof, S., Giuliano, F., Martin, M., May, K., … Morris, M. (2007b). Development and validation of a premature ejaculation diagnostic tool. *European Urology, 52*(5), 565–573.

Symonds, T., Roblin, D., Hart, K., & Althof, S. (2003). How does premature ejaculation impact a man's life. *Journal of Sex and Marital Therapy, 29*(5), 361–370.

Taylor, G. J., Bagby, R. M., & Parker, J. D. A. (1999). *Disorders of affect regulation: Alexithymia in medical and psychiatric illness.* New York: Cambridge University Press.

Teyber, E. (1997). *Interpersonal process in psychotherapy: A relational approach.* Pacific Grove, CA: Brooks Cole.

Tondo, L., Cantone, M., Carta, M., & Laddomada, A. (1991). An MMPI evaluation of male sexual dysfunction. *Journal of Clinical Psychology, 47,* 391–396.

Tsitouras, P. D., & Alvarez, R. R. (1984). Etiology and management of sexual dysfunction in elderly men. *Psychiatric Medicine, 2,* 43–55.

Vale, J. (1999). Ejaculatory dysfunction. *British Journal of Urology International, 83,* 557–563.

Waldinger, M. D., Rietschel, M., Nothen, M., Hengeveld, M. W., & Olivier, B. (1997). Familial occurrence of primary premature ejaculation. *Psychiatric Genetics, 8,* 37–40.

Wincze, J. P., & Carey, M. P. (1991). *Sexual dysfunction: A guide for assessment and treatment.* New York: The Guilford Press.

Witt, M. A., & Grantmyre, J. E. (1993). Ejaculatory failure. *World Journal of Urology, 11,* 89–95.

Zilbergeld, B. (1993). *The new male sexuality.* New York: Bantam Books.

9

Appendix: Tools and Resources

Appendix 1

Useful Addresses

Clinically-Oriented Sexuality Associations

These associations provide continuing education related to the treatment of sexual problems.

International Society for Sexual Medicine (ISSM)
PO Box 94
1520 AB Wormerveer
The Netherlands
Tel. +31 75 647-6372
Web: http://www.issm.info

Society for Sex Therapy Research (SSTAR)
6311 W. Gross Point Road
Niles, IL 60714
USA
Tel. +1 847 647-8832
Web: http://www.sstarnet.org

American Urological Association (AUA)
1000 Corporate Boulevard
Linthicum, MD 21090
USA
Tel. +1 410 689-3700
Web: http://www.auanet.org

Society for the Scientific Study of Sexuality (SSSS)
PO Box 416
Allentown, PA 18105
USA
Tel. +1 610 443-3100
Web: http://www.sexscience.org

American Association for Sex Educators, Counselors and Therapists (AASECT)
PO Box 1960
Ashland, VA 23005-1960
USA
Tel. +1 804 752-0026
Web: http://www.aasect.org

American Society of Andrology
1100 E. Woodfield Road, Suite 520
Schaumburg, IL 60173
USA
Tel. +1 847-619-4909
Web: http://www.andrologysociety.com

Appendix 2

Male Sexual Functioning Questionnaires and Surveys

International Index of Erectile Function (IIEF)
http://www.urologyspecialists.net/print/iief.html

Sexual Health Inventory for Men (SHIM)
http://www.rohbaltimore.com/SHIM.pdf

Self-Esteem and Relationship Questionnaire (SEAR)
(can be found in Cappelleri et al., 2004)

Male Sexual Health Questionnaire (MSHQ)
(questions can be found in Rosen et al., 2004a)

Premature Ejaculation Prevalence and Attitudes (PEPA)
(can be found in Patrick et al., 2005, p. 361)

Index of Premature Ejaculation (IPE)
(can be found in Althof et al., 2006, pp. 474–475, but the material is copyrighted and requires special access)

Premature Ejaculation Diagnostic Tool (PEDT)
http://www.urosource.com/fileadmin/European_Urology/New_Releases08/Giuliano_April__early_release.pdf

Quality of Erection Questionnaire (QEQ)
http://prolutssh.com/articles/QEQ-Porst.pdf

Sexual Quality of Life Measure for Men
Available through the Patient Reported Outcomes in Lower Urinary Tract Symptoms (LUTS) and Sexual Health website at http://www.prolutssh.com/index.html

IIEF, SHIM, SEAR, IPE, PEDT, QEQ, SQOL as well as other questionnaires about male sexual dysfunction are available at http://www.prolutssh.com

Appendix 3

Typical Starting Questions for Identifying a Sexual Dysfunction

Initial question	Sample elaborations
Do you ...	
Have sexual interests, desires, thoughts, fantasies?	What is your masturbation frequency?
	Who is the initiator of intercourse?
	What is your level of interest or attraction to your partner?
Have difficulty getting or keeping an erection?	What is the frequency of coital impairment? Do you experience a loss of erection before ejaculating?
	What is the degree of your erection (none, some, etc.)?
Ejaculate before you wish?	Do you ejaculate before intercourse begins?
	Do you ejaculate within 1 or 2 min after penetration?
	Are you able to delay or postpone ejaculation? Do you ejaculate for fear of losing erection?
Take longer than you wish to reach orgasm?	Do you ever ejaculate, e.g., during masturbation? What is your ratio of orgasms to attempts?
	What is the duration of intercourse?
Have pain during intercourse?	Do you experience pain before, during, or after?

Note. [a]These prototypical items are meant only as conversation starters that help narrow the problem to a specific domain. A full assessment would include a complete psychosexual history and evaluation.
Adapted from "Sexual Health and Problems: Erectile Dysfunction, Premature Ejaculation, and Orgasmic Disorders," by D. L. Rowland, in J. Grant & M. Potenza (Eds.), *Textbook of Men's Mental Health* (pp. 171–204). Arlington, VA: American Psychiatric Association Press, 2007.